face2face

Praise for *Face2Face*

"Need to know how to be authentic online? Want to interact with the public smartly, safely, and successfully? This book is going to be vital to your social media success."

—Kathy Dempsey, marketing
consultant, Libraries Are Essential

"An informative and much needed resource for business owners."

—Joe Cheray, Wildheart Social Media

"*Face2Face* is the perfect book to help an organization become part of and stay aware of the conversations happening about them online. David Lee King lays out both tools and strategies that can be used immediately to start having better conversations with your customers."

—Jason Griffey, author,
Mobile Technology and Libraries

"There is a difference between knowing how to work a social media service and knowing how to get that service to work for you. This book gives you the skills to bridge that gap."

—Michael P. Sauers, author,
Blogging and RSS, Second Edition

"David Lee King shares the key tips for creating the community connections that make the modern socially networked organization successful."

—Joe Murphy, www.joemurphylibraryfuture.com

"*Face2Face* is a solid primer for businesses looking to be more social. Following King's advice will lead to increased business and greater customer loyalty."

—Patrick O'Keefe, iFroggy Network,
and author, *Managing Online Forums*

"David Lee King does it again! His leadership in experimenting with new social tools blazes the trail rather than following the pack."

—Stephen Abram MLS,
VP, Gale Cengage Learning

face2face

Using Facebook, Twitter, and Other Social Media
Tools to Create Great Customer Connections

David Lee King

CyberAge Books

Information Today, Inc.
Medford, New Jersey

First printing, 2012

Face2Face: Using Facebook, Twitter, and Other Social Media Tools to Create Great Customer Connections

Publisher's Note: The author and publisher have taken care in preparation of this book but make no expressed or implied warranty of any kind and assume no responsibility for errors or omissions. No liability is assumed for incidental or consequential damages in connection with or arising out of the use of the information or programs contained herein.

Many of the designations used by manufacturers and sellers to distinguish their products are claimed as trademarks. Where those designations appear in this book and Information Today, Inc. was aware of a trademark claim, the designations have been printed with initial capital letters.

Library of Congress Cataloging-in-Publication Data

King, David Lee, 1966-
  Face2Face : using Facebook, Twitter, and other social media tools to create great customer connections / by David Lee King.
    p. cm.
Includes index.
ISBN 978-0-910965-99-6
1. Online social networks/ 2. Business networks. 3. Customer relations. I. Title. II. Title: Face to face.
HM742.K56 2012
302.30285--dc23

                                                        2012013506

President and CEO: Thomas H. Hogan, Sr.
Editor-in-Chief and Publisher: John B. Bryans
VP Graphics and Production: M. Heide Dengler
Managing Editor: Amy M. Reeve
Project Editor: Rachel Singer Gordon
Editorial Assistant: Brandi Scardilli
Cover Designer: Lisa Conroy
Copyeditor: Dorothy Pike
Proofreader: Barbara Brynko
Indexer: Kathleen Rocheleau

www.infotoday.com

CONTENTS

126981

ACKNOWLEDGMENTS

I want to thank the following people—without them, this book wouldn't exist.

First of all, thanks to Rachel Singer Gordon, my editor, and John Bryans, editor-in-chief of the Books Division at Information Today, Inc., for pestering me about writing a second book: "So David, have you started thinking about your next book yet?" … "Hey David, just wondering if you've thought about writing another book?" …

Thanks to my awesome wife, Dana. She puts up with all my shenanigans ("So, why exactly do you need another guitar, David?") and my hours spent in front of the laptop, typing away. She also read through the whole manuscript—proofing, editing, and improving—even before I sent the manuscript to Rachel.

And, thanks to YOU. I get ideas from you guys—in tweets, in videos, in blog posts, in conversations, in presentations, or during a shared dinner. Without you, this book would not exist.

You guys ROCK.

ABOUT DAVID'S BLOG

www.davidleeking.com/face2face

David blogs at www.davidleeking.com, where he writes about the intersection of social media and emerging trends. More information about this book can be found at www.davidleeking.com/face 2face, and in individual posts, which can be found at www.david leeking.com/category/face2face.

INTRODUCTION

I recently bought a RØDE VideoMic Pro. This is a way-cool microphone created specifically for improving the sound in videos. It has a camera shoe connection, so it can sit on top of a camcorder or a DSLR camera, and it provides great sound.

While researching this microphone, I visited RØDE's website and discovered that the company is doing a lot with social media. RØDE has both Twitter and Facebook accounts, so I followed and friended the company. Soon after, someone from RØDE direct messaged me in Twitter, saying: "Hey thanks for following! Please fire any questions, suggestions, praise, &/or abuse you have at us, we would love to hear from you!" [Author's Note: All quotes from social media included in this book are shown as is, complete with misspellings.]

That's just the beginning of how RØDE seems to work hard at interacting with its customers. For example, the company recently asked its Twitter followers this question: "We're going to rock this weekend!! tell us who/what/where/when/how you're going to rock with RØDE Microphones!! #rockwithrode."[1]

The people at RØDE also answer questions and give advice via Twitter. One Twitter follower, @RichardHall93, tweeted: "Good wedding today. Gutted that @rodemics VideoMic Pro's quality is so poor. Broken on it's 2nd outing. http://t.co/0NPOvra"[2]

RØDE read Richard's comment and responded with some great customer support: "Hi Richard, all our mics are covered by a 10 Year Warranty—pls email worldsupport@rodemic.com, they can send you a new part."[3]

RØDE staff keep track of questions their customers ask and sometimes follow up via Twitter. Here's one example of a typical follow-up response: "@legitimatelouis We sent you a tweet a few days ago http://bit.ly/eaqUpx—does that answer your question or do you need more info?"[4]

Remove the "social media hipness" of Twitter for a second, and what is RØDE doing? Providing great customer service. Conversations between customers and a company are taking place, and these sound very much like what you might overhear at a local mom-and-pop photography store. Real people working at RØDE are following up with their customers to make sure those customers are happy with RØDE products and that they have the answers they need.

RØDE provides a great example of customer service and support via Twitter—one that more organizations would do well to emulate. What's the problem? Some organizations simply don't know where to start.

That's why I wrote this book.

Many people already understand how to personally connect with friends and family using 21st-century tools like Facebook or Twitter. Facebook lets me easily stay in touch with my nephew, who lives six states away, and I can even connect with interesting "people I once knew"—like all the people I went to high school with who recently friended me because our 25th high school reunion was coming up.

This part's easy—you click Like and move on, right? Simple stuff.

When we try to take those same social media tools and use them to connect our organizations to our customers, though, it becomes much more difficult. Many organizations have struggled to understand how to interact with customers online. Because these organizations don't understand how online connections work, they have had to "learn under fire"—some even by making their first leap into social media via an apology video on YouTube, like JetBlue's CEO did a couple of years ago (www.youtube.com/watch?v=-r_PI7EAUw).

Today, the average business or organization has yet to embrace emerging social tools and many haven't even started. Yes, they do have websites, but the content is mostly about the organization itself—there are no face2face connections taking place between customers and the organization. Do they use social tools like Facebook or Twitter? Rarely. If they are using these tools, they are using them primarily as a one-way broadcast medium, not as a way to connect with customers and deepen customer relationships.

These organizations are still planning for traditional business-as-usual physical interactions and relying on traditional tools like press releases, advertisements, and marketing write-ups. Their customers, however, are using social media tools like blogs, Twitter, Facebook, or YouTube to talk about those companies, their products, and their services. They want face2face interactions online, just like they want them when visiting an organization's physical space.

What are these organizations missing? They are missing a face2face presence on their websites. They are missing conversations and community. These organizations need to start holding conversations—in Twitter's 140 characters or less—and follow up by responding to mentions and "retweets." The conversation needs to continue in blog posts, status updates, and comment boxes. These conversations can be made visual with the use of multimedia—by using pictures of products on Flickr or a video on YouTube.

My goal in this book is to help organizations learn how face2face works in an organizational setting. To meet that goal, we will explore how organizations can connect with people in a variety of online settings. Readers will find plenty of examples of what's currently working and what's not.

Here's what you'll find in this book.

Chapter 1 contains an explanation in general terms of what it means to be "human" on the web—how communication, listening, and sharing in online communities can make an organization seem "human."

Chapter 2 discusses how the web is changing the way we communicate and explains how to use social media tools to communicate in a more natural, inviting way.

Chapter 3 explores how you can use images and videos as visual tools to connect with your customers. You will also find tips about how to most effectively use pictures and videos organizationally.

Grassroots online communities can form around products, services, organizations, and ideas. In Chapter 4, I'll explain how these types of communities form, share some handy tools that can be used to help support these online communities, and in the process, provide some ways your organization can have a human touch while interacting with customers in these community-driven spaces.

In Chapter 5, we'll look at what online listening entails; describe some ways for organizations to listen to conversations online, like what to listen for and how and when to respond; and finally, we'll look at some online listening tools.

Being formal is the fastest way to kill the personal touch in corporate communications to customers. Your customers want you to be human. Chapter 6 explains how to let your organization's "personality" hang out a bit to help your customers feel comfortable connecting with you.

Friendly, open design can be inviting and can help customers feel welcome in a physical space. This principle also holds true online. Chapter 7 explores how a well-designed digital experience can help your organization provide that face2face human touch for customers.

Chapter 8 focuses on tools like blogs, Facebook, Twitter, and YouTube. We will discuss what you can do with each tool to connect your organization to your customers and how to make human connections while using each service.

Your organization will have critics. Chapter 9 explains how to handle criticism online.

Want to know where to start? Chapter 10 gives you some starting tips and focuses on creating strategy and goals.

In Chapter 11, I focus on measurement and analytics tools, and answer some questions, including: Why measure? What can be measured? How can you measure?

And finally, Chapter 12 is the "application" chapter. We are going to take some of what we learned throughout the book and apply it to a business setting to see how making face2face connections works in the real world.

Endnotes

1. Rodemics, Twitter post, accessed January 16, 2012, www.twitter.com/#!/rodemics/status/64077629443158016.

2. RichardHall93, Twitter post, accessed January 16, 2012, www.twitter.com/#!/RichardHall93/status/61565597162553344.

3. Rodemics, Twitter post, accessed January 16, 2012, www.twitter.com/#!/rodemics/status/63733103646085120.

4. Rodemics, Twitter post, accessed January 16, 2012, www.twitter.com/#!/rodemics/status/60120777948803072.

CHAPTER 1

Face2Face on the Web

What Makes You Human on the Web?

"Being human" online is hard to define, isn't it? Sometimes we "connect" with a company online, but we have a hard time describing why it seems approachable. When searching Google for ideas for this chapter, I had to try a few different phrases before I discovered what I really wanted to find. First, I tried *being human on the web*, which didn't get me too far (bad search syntax, David—bad, bad, bad). Then I tried *being real online*, which led to *being authentic online*.

Scanning through the results of those searches, I finally started finding content that resonated. Even then, I had to wade through some highly irrelevant content. For example, I found some "great" articles on how to figure out if the prospects found on dating sites were being real or if they were lying. I also found at least one clothing store that wanted you to "be real" with your fashion sense—and it also wanted you to buy its pricey, glitzy clothing.

But wading through all that information was helpful, because I also found some really useful discussions on using an authentic voice online, or how *not* to use corporate speak. That was more like it.

So, back to my original question: What makes you human on the web?

Being "human" or "real" in an online setting is an emerging idea, especially for organizations and businesses that can't hire experts to connect with customers online. For these organizations, the idea of being real online can be rather daunting. There are still organizations that don't have a web presence or are just starting out in representing themselves online. For those organizations, just being online is challenging enough. When you add in the even newer concept of social media, or of marketing as a conversation, that becomes even more daunting.

All of this is very new. For some small businesses, even thinking about a computer that connects to more than their inventory database is a pretty new concept. When you combine the fear of the unknown with open internet access and customers leaving potentially nasty comments everywhere, interacting online can be a scary new world for some.

Transform Your Organization Into a Face2Face Organization

How can we take on this online challenge? For starters, let's examine three general concepts of being human, or authentic, in online settings. These three concepts—listening, authentic communication, and sharing in a community—are already implemented in our stores or offices, so let's apply them online, too.

Listening

I listed listening first, because this is the very first thing you should do for your business in an online setting. We'll cover listening in more detail in Chapter 5, but let's introduce the concept now—it's that important!

You've probably always listened to customer comments in your business (or should have, anyway). When a business creates a new product to sell, someone first does market research to gauge interest. When a nonprofit organization introduces a new service, this is often because constituents have voiced a need. In each case, the organization listens to its current or potential customers, offers a product or service, and then listens to feedback about the offering and adjusts it accordingly.

What about those times when a customer enters a business or restaurant or library, has a less-than-stellar experience, and wants to complain? Same thing happens: You listen to the complaint. Good organizations will cut through the frustration, listen to the core of the customer's criticism or complaint, apologize, and try to make the customer's experience a better one. If other customers have similar complaints, the organization will probably work to fix the issue. That is basic customer service, right? But it's also basic listening.

This type of listening also works great on the web—possibly even better than in-person listening. Why? Because on the web, you have multiple ways to "eavesdrop" on your customers and learn their thoughts about your product or service!

Some of your customers are probably using social media tools like Twitter or Facebook, or have created personal blogs. Each of these online social tools creates a voice for people. If those people are talking about you, your business or organization, and the stuff

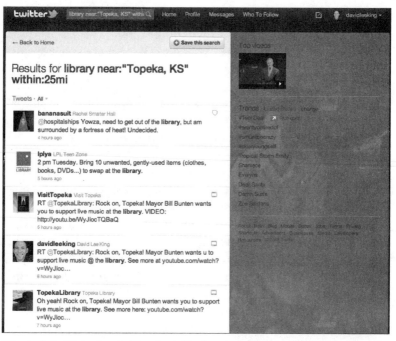

Figure 1.1   Listening to Topeka talk about its library via Twitter Search

you do, guess what? You can easily "listen in" on the conversation taking place and can quickly gauge what your customers think about you—without having to wait for them to come to your store or office space. Simply set up search alerts for your organization's name (learn how in Chapter 5). Figure 1.1 is an example of a library using Twitter as a listening tool.

This type of listening can get visual and audible, too, through the use of online photo and video services. Want to see someone unbox your new product? Go directly to YouTube or Flickr. Want to see someone complain about the same product he just unboxed, after discovering something he doesn't like about it? Or praise your new product because it's just the thing he needed? You can see all of these types of things online.

Get started on listening by setting up searches, subscribing to some RSS feeds, and creating some email alerts. Your customers have much to say, but they're not necessarily saying it directly to you. When they talk about you, they are talking to each other—to other customers. You need to be in on those conversations, too.

Authentic Communication

After you have created some listening channels, you simply need to respond. But there's a caveat—you need to respond authentically! I like what Taylor Hill at Harkins Creative says about creating an authentic voice:[1]

1. Be a giver. Give of yourself by providing good solid information about what you do or the products you represent. If you think it's the same old information that everyone else is giving away then put your own spin to it with a good true story or analogy. Don't be afraid of putting yourself and your company out there; sometimes it's the only way to get the conversation going.

2. Be yourself. Everyone is unique, and it's that uniqueness that enables each of us to see something from our own point of view. Giving your take on something should always be conversational even if it is different or even confrontational. As long as you always remember that this is a conversation with one or more people who are all a part of the exchange, then civil discourse can take place.

Taylor defines being a "giver" as providing good, solid information about your products or services—or even your organization's thoughts about the industry. You're not trying to mask an inadequacy; you're not trying to put a spin on something. Instead, you are merely sharing what you think, how you think a product should be used, or what it is you do.

Taylor also suggests that to create an authentic voice, you should let your unique voice be heard. The unique way we think and how we say things helps us come across as authentic, which makes us seem "more human" online.

To start creating an authentic-sounding voice online, you need to develop conversational, authentic ways to communicate with customers and constituents, rather than edit all the quirks and uniqueness out of your organizational communications. Don't try to turn your online interactions into corporate speak. When you edit out all those quirks, you have sterilized your message—not a good idea if you want to sound authentic online.

This concept doesn't apply exclusively to text-based communication, either. Today's communication paths include everything from text- to image- to audio- to video-based communication. At the library where I work, I've blogged, but I've also created videos to communicate messages. I've been on the evening news. We have a regular podcast to share "what's happening at the library." I have taken photos of a new service to share with our customers. I've even made a screencast to show how a new website works.

The point here? I'm communicating online textually, visually, and aurally—through words, sight, and sound. In each of these settings, I need to create an authentic voice. We'll discuss how to do just that in later chapters.

Sharing in Online Community

Now that we've covered listening and communicating with an authentic voice, let's take it on the road.

In other words, take your message to other websites. It's one thing to communicate via your own blog on your own website, where you can control your message—and somewhat control the comments and responses that might pour in. It's quite another thing to jump into an online social network, say those same things, and start participating in an active, online community forum setting with your customers.

Authenticity is even more important in these settings. Why? Because people can and will call you out if you don't get this right. It's certainly happened before. For example, back in 2009, Honda's Facebook Page for its Crosstour SUV received a lot of comments—many negative—about the visual design of the car. During the ongoing discussion, one "customer" named Eddie Okubo chimed in and said, "Interesting design. I would get this car in a heartbeat. I may be the older crowd with my kids out of the house and still need some space and performance. Don't need anything big."

However, there was an authenticity problem here. Eddie happened to be the manager of product planning at Honda—but he didn't mention that fact. Honda's customers called him out. One customer responded by saying, "Sounds like you are trying to save your job at Honda?" and another said, "Maybe you like it Eddie because you're the MANAGER OF PRODUCT PLANNING at Honda (light trucks in particular)? Lol!"

Honda officials responded by deleting Eddie's comment from the Facebook Page and responded with this: "Eddie Okubo is a manager in Honda Product Planning. His post was removed for two reasons: 1) He did not first state that he is a Honda employee and that his posting is his personal—not Honda's—opinion, and 2) he is not a spokesperson for Honda."[2]

What do you think? Was Eddie wrong to post that comment? Well, yes and no. We really don't know if Eddie believed what he said about the Crosstour or not. Personally, I hope he did—it's pretty cool when employees at a company actually like the products they help create. There's nothing wrong with that at all. However, Eddie should have disclosed that he worked for Honda and that he helped design the car. Would that have subtracted from his comment? Probably not. He could have found an authentic way to state that: 1) He helped design it, and 2) he loves the design and would buy the car himself.

There's a third aspect to this story, though. Did Honda handle this PR situation correctly? Again, yes and no. Yes, the company needed to be very up-front with customers, especially customers in a public forum. (An open Facebook Page is most definitely a public forum!) So Honda did all right by admitting that Eddie worked for the company and was only sharing his personal opinion.

However, Honda erred by stating that Eddie "is not a spokesperson for Honda." Why? Because every single person who works at Honda is a spokesperson for Honda. If you work somewhere and tell friends, relatives, and acquaintances that you love your job (or you hate your job because of a bad boss that the company won't fire), you are a spokesperson. When you help create a new product and share the joys and thrills of being part of that with friends at a party, you are a spokesperson. You're not the official "I'm in the PR department, and I make the official statements for the company" type of spokesperson … but you are a spokesperson nonetheless.

The concept of being a spokesperson is changing. It has gone from hiring a PR department that handles all official communications to having an organization's normal, everyday employees sharing what they think—about what they do, what they create, and where they work—online, in social networks. Sharing that type of information is now as easy as typing a sentence and hitting the Send button.

Instead of deleting posts and trying to control the message, Honda could train its employees on the appropriate ways to communicate—including using proper identification and disclosures—and then set them free to connect and share what they like about the company's products. Allowing employees to be part of the conversation can go a long way toward building an authentic, unique voice for an organization. It will help make your organizational voice personal, unique, and authentic. It will help you connect face2face with your online customers.

That's what the rest of this book is about. So let's consider the how-to's of being authentic online.

Endnotes

1. Taylor Hill, "3 Steps to Being Transparent and Developing an Authentic Voice Online," The Agency Record Blog, accessed January 17, 2012, www.harkins creative.com/3-steps-to-being-transparent-and-developing-an-authentic-voice-online.

2. Jonny Lieberman, "Honda Purges Select Comments From Crosstour Facebook Page," Autoblog, September 3, 2009, accessed January 17, 2012, www.autoblog. com/2009/09/03/honda-purges-some-comments-from-crosstour-facebook-page.

Face2Face Communication

While visiting Spain to do some speaking a few years ago, I kept in touch with my wife and kids through iChat. The call itself was free, since iChat is web-based—I just had to pay for internet access at the hotel (which I was using for other reasons anyway).

iChat worked great. I had my trusty MacBook Pro with me, which has a built-in microphone and webcam. At home, we have an iMac with a similar setup. So instead of having to strap something on our heads, we turned on the webcams at each end, I placed the call, and *voilà*! I was talking to—and seeing—my lovely wife and my kids. We communicated essentially for free, over the internet, continents away.

Even now—3 years later—I still think that's pretty darn cool!

Even though my family's *medium* of communication was new and amazing, what we were really doing was as old as time. Humans have been communicating quite well for a very long time. Communication is simply part of what we do—it's part of being human.

These days, we communicate in many different ways. We talk: in person, on the phone (whether you are talking or texting), or over Skype. Visually, we can communicate our message via photos, videos, or even drawings. Writing can look traditional, like this book. But the medium might look nontraditional—you may be reading via a computer screen, phone text, smartphone, or even a Kindle or an iPad. Until recently, people generally communicated through standard, traditional tools, like the phone, TV, or a letter. (In this day and age, email could even be grouped into that more traditional form, too.) Modern, emerging web technology, however, has been morphing those traditional communication paths. For example, people still use the phone, but they might also use Skype to accomplish the same type of communication.

We can also communicate using web-based tools. Blogging is one type of communication tool. Blogging is great because it's essentially a writer's tool. The writer can focus on anything, from an individual simply keeping an online personal journal to a Fortune 500 company sharing the next steps for its flagship product. The same blogging tool has many different uses.

Blogging and social networks are great ways to communicate via the web. Since you may already be somewhat acquainted with blogging and social networks, let's start there. The rest of this chapter will take an in-depth look at blogging and social media tools. More specifically, we'll look at how to communicate and connect with your customers via an organizational blog or organization-based social media tools.

Two Bloggers

Chris Brogan

Chris Brogan is a well-known blogger who writes about emerging business communication, social media, and marketing. His main blog (www.chrisbrogan.com) is very popular among those interested in marketing and social media, and Chris does a great job of connecting with his readers.

How does he do this? Simple: He asks. For example, in his post "11 Free Resources About Creativity,"[1] he asks his readers a question at the end of the post: "What's your take? What values are you adding to your community by helping them curate and find the good stuff? How are you helping your community grow with this information?"

By adding questions at the end of most of his blog posts, Chris is inviting his readers to add their thoughts. And they do—as of March 2012, this particular blog post had received 49 comments, 200 Facebook Likes, and 565 Twitter reactions so far. Not bad for a three-paragraph article.

Bill Marriott

Bill Marriott of Marriott Hotels also blogs (www.blogs.marriott.com). He also seems to connect to people, judging by the number of comments he's receiving. Bill, however, doesn't tend to ask questions. Instead, he shares how much he cares about the hotel industry and about Marriott Hotels and staff. He basically writes about the business end of his company, focusing on things like a new loyalty program or hotel restaurants.

You can tell he cares about his customers and his business by the tone he uses. He often uses phrases like "We're having a lot of fun" or mentions tidbits like the fact that he personally visited over 300 hotels in 2010. Bill cares about his hotels, and his readers notice. People are connecting to him, to his blog, and to Marriott hotels in the process.

Chris and Bill each connect to their readers via blog content. In both cases (especially with Bill), that connection equals a connection to the organizations they represent. Bill creates a connection to Marriott, and Chris to his many business ventures. That connection, though, is more than just readers responding to well-written content. That's certainly part of it, but the human connection Chris and Bill make with their readers through their content is even more important.

How to Make Your Blog Human

Chris and Bill primarily use written, blog-based communication to connect with their readers, including current and potential customers. How can you use a blog to make face2face human connections to your readers and customers? The following sections outline a variety of simple techniques to help you begin.

Use Conversational Writing

The first way to make your blog sound human is to use conversational language. Write as if you're having a conversation with a friend. For example, on my own blog (www.davidleeking.com), I use "you" when I talk to readers. This helps bring the person into the conversation—and, because it is a conversation, it's natural to say "you" when I'm talking to *you*. When I'm talking to you in person, I might ask: "Did you like that restaurant?" or "What do you think about the rough draft of my chapter?"

It's the same thing with a blog post. Blog posts are not the same type of communication as your corporate report. Instead, they are the start of a written conversation. Use the same tools you would use when talking to someone in person; it's just a typed conversation instead of a spoken one. Another way to think about it is that you should write using casual rather than formal language. Think business casual. Or if it helps, pretend that you're writing to a friend in the industry. That can help keep the conversation, well, conversational (more how-to's in a second).

Also try to be succinct. Think of your blog post as if you're "forcing the conversation" just a bit. Be quick to come to the point. You may only have a few seconds to catch your reader's interest before he clicks away—so, no rambling allowed.

Encourage Commenting to Continue the Conversation

A couple of years ago, I wrote a blog post titled "Am I a 2.0 Librarian and the Library 2.0 Spectrum."[2] In the post, I was thinking "out loud" about some emerging skill sets for librarians who work on the web. That blog post garnered a lot of comments—26 of them— and actually pushed me to write multiple posts, revising my first thoughts based on the comments I received.

Here's how the conversation went:

1. My original post with a graphic illustrating my point (Figure 2.1)

2. The next post, which asked for help based on the comments I received, to make the idea better

3. The third post, which shared more thoughts stemming from the discussion

4. The last post, which included a new graphic based on all the comments I received from the first three posts (Figure 2.2)

The point here is that I threw out the first idea as a conversation starter. Other people continued the conversation by commenting on my blog post. Then, I responded by updating my idea and by including other people's thoughts in the process. My first post was the start of the conversation—not the end of the conversation.

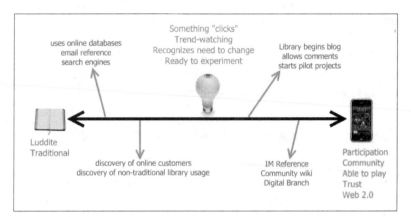

Figure 2.1   Library 2.0 Spectrum

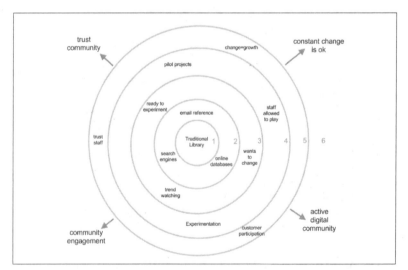

Figure 2.2   Library 2.0 Ripples

The comments were just as important, if not more so, as the original post.

In blog form, true conversation cannot happen without comments. It's sort of like a conversation at a coffeeshop or with a friend or colleague. If you're the only one talking, it's not a conversation—it's a diatribe or soliloquy! But when others chime in and share their thoughts or reactions to what you said, that turns the blog post into an actual conversation ... and makes it much more interesting in the process.

What If It Gets Ugly?

Most conversations are usually pretty neutral and harmless, especially when focused on work projects. Even when something goes wrong with a product or service, people are mostly civil. But not always, right? I'm sure you've encountered a hostile customer or co-worker at some point during your career.

What should you do if the conversation gets ugly in the comments section of your blog post? Generally, you'll want to do the same thing you'd do if a physical conversation got ugly. With an in-person conversation, you might retreat, regroup, ignore, and move on, or perhaps try to steer the conversation back on topic. Each of these tactics works online, too.

Luckily for you, though, online, guided conversations—such as the conversations happening in the comments of your organization's blog post—can be a bit more manageable than real life. Why? Because you can have a comments policy.

Facebook and Flickr both have useful, usable comment policies, and similar policies will work well for blogs, too. For example, Facebook's Terms page includes these points under Safety:[3]

- You will not bully, intimidate, or harass any user.

- You will not post content that: is hateful, threatening, or pornographic; incites violence; or contains nudity or graphic or gratuitous violence.

Flickr includes similar language regarding the responsibilities of users; things like this:[4]

- Do play nice. We're a community of many types of people, who all have the right to feel comfortable and who may not think what you think, believe what you believe or see what you see. So, be polite and respectful in your interactions with other members.

- Don't vent your frustrations, rant, or bore the brains out of other members. Flickr is not a venue for you to harass, abuse, impersonate, or intimidate others. If we receive a valid complaint about your conduct, we'll send you a warning or delete your account.

- Don't be creepy. You know the guy. Don't be that guy.

My own place of work has adapted some of that language, and we have used it specifically for commenting on our blog posts. Following my employer's Community Discussion Guidelines;[5] these are placed at the bottom of every blog post, beside the comment box:

> Here are some guidelines to posting comments and content at Topeka & Shawnee County Public Library's digital branch. The goal? To help you have fun!

We encourage comments:

- We want to hear from you! Please post comments, questions, and other thoughts … as you think them. That's why we're here.

- Stay on topic. Stick to the subject and issues raised by the post, not the person who made it or others who commented on it.

- Think before you press the publish button. Remember that this is a public forum, and your words will be archived on this site and available for anyone to find for a long time—the web has a very long memory.

- If you can't be polite, don't say it. Respect is the name of the game. You must respect your fellow commenters.

Some don'ts:

- Don't post copyrighted materials (articles, videos, audio, etc.) that you do not have permission to reproduce or distribute.

- Don't post content that installs viruses, worms, malware, trojans, etc.

- Don't post content that is obscene, libelous, defamatory, or hateful.

- Don't post spam.

- Don't post personal, real-life information such as home addresses and home phone numbers.

What will we do?

- We'll respond to comments, answer questions, and provide suggestions as appropriate.

- Sometimes we'll join a comment thread to help focus (or refocus) the discussion or to get people talking.

- If you break one of the guidelines above (or come close to it), we'll email you and ask you to stop. We might also post a reminder to the discussion. If it continues, we will delete your comments and block you from posting.

- We will remove any posts that are obviously commercial or otherwise spam-like.

- We will remove content that puts us in legal jeopardy, such as potentially libelous or defamatory postings, or material posted in potential breach of copyright.

As you can see from these examples, the goals in comment guidelines are simple. In each case, when a commenter has a brief moment of insanity and acts up on your website, you can simply point to your guidelines. Say "Dude, you can't do this here" and deal with the problem by deleting the comment, editing it, or even blocking a user's account if necessary. Remember, though, that blocking a user is a last resort. Give a warning first and try to anticipate problems up-front, in hopes that you *don't* have to edit or delete people's comments. They want to share, and you really don't want to put a damper on the party before the party begins.

Above all, remember this: Always be nice. Yes, this means you. You're the one in charge of the conversation, so it simply makes sense for you to be a bit above reproach. Be nice to your readers— even if they're nasty.

People can also be uglier on the web than in real life (sort of like with road rage)—especially people not used to the whole connecting-with-others concept. If you create a blog that attracts readers, you will encounter mean people. Get over it and move on. Life's too short to get uptight about those few exceptions. Many times, the best thing to do when dealing with really negative people is to simply ignore them. On the web, ignoring someone is pretty much equal to saying, "Your contribution isn't valuable; go away." Ouch.

Lastly, remember this: Even if you receive a less-than-stellar comment, this means that you connected with someone, and even got a reaction. Those people took time to comment, so you have met your goal of communicating face2face.

Add Pictures to Your Content

Adding pictures to your content helps others connect with the content, with the writer, and with the organization. A while ago, I read that bloggers should add pictures to their blog posts, so I started doing it. In my post titled "Rethinking the 3rd Place"[6]—an interesting concept about where customers spend their time (work and home are places one and two ... your goal is to be the third place)—I added an image of a coffee cup with a heart shape in the bubbles of the coffee (Figure 2.3) to support the concept of a third place (since a coffee shop is often considered to be a "third place" for many people).

Here's a comment I received about that post, related to the image, from Marlene:

> My comment is not as a professional librarian.
>
> As someone whose learning style includes a strong visual component I must say I love [that] coffeecup heart image!
>
> Just seeing it prompts me to read with an open heart and mind what comes next.

Figure 2.3   Coffee shop as a third place

Visual communication is much more than direct corollary to meaning for me it's learning prep, setting an environment for meaningful intellectual exchange.

Maybe you just liked the image—I just liked the feeling and now commit to actually reading the post.

Beyond enjoying the image I ordered your book and am wondering how I missed its launch last year?

Marlene explains well the reasons to include images (and hey, she went out and bought my last book, too!). Including an image with your text, if it supports the concepts in the post, can add a lot to the meaning. Images can also visually demonstrate your topic. For example, in another post from my website, titled "10 Tips to Do Presentations Like Me: Use Presenter View,"[7] I inserted a photograph into the blog post of my laptop screen during a presentation to actually show what my presenter view looks like.

The photo visually demonstrates and supports what I was writing about in the text of the post. Readers have two ways to figure out what I mean: They can read the article, or they can simply look at the accompanying image and get some useful information from that alone.

Here's what Darren Rowse, who blogs about blogging at www.problogger.net, says about adding images to blog posts:[8] "I'm a big believer in catching the attention of readers by whatever means is needed—picture, keyword, intriguing title, promise of free gifts (ok—not that one—yet). I got to look at some Eyetools results for one of my blogs recently and was intrigued to see how pictures inside a longer article can actually help to draw readers eyes down the page. Very useful strategy. It's all part of making your blog scannable—drawing your reader in—grabbing their attention."

Images are great. Respecting copyright is also great. When choosing an image for your blog post, do one of two things:

1. Use your own image. If you know how to take photographs or create web-ready images or graphics, do so—and use them to accompany your blog post.

2. Use Creative Commons images. Creative Commons is a simple way to grant extended fair use licenses to people wanting to use your work for their purposes. For example, let's say I want to use someone's Creative Commons licensed photo of a magnifying glass in my library's blog post about new spy novels. If the photographer has added a Creative Commons license to her photograph, she has granted me permission to use that photograph—in advance. I don't have to ask! Be sure to credit the content creator, however; many Creative Commons licenses require attribution.

Where can you find photographs that use a Creative Commons license? Here are two places to start:

- Creative Commons Search, search.creativecommons.org
- Flickr's Explore Creative Commons, www.flickr.com/creativecommons

Both of these search engines will help you find photographs with a Creative Commons license attached.

Images and photos work. They do three essential things:

1. Pictures humanize a blog post. Your image choices help people get to know the writer and the organization a little better. They also help your readers connect to your writing, thus helping them connect that much more to *you*. (Pictures of yourself do that even more—they add a face to the voice.)

2. Pictures draw people into the content. As Darren Rowse pointed out, images actually help draw people's eyes down the page. So, including an image can help your written content get read. An interesting photo or graphic that supports the idea of the post will draw people further into your content.

3. Pictures help people decipher the content. Pictures can add value to a post by making the post more understandable. They can illustrate the text and the ideas. Pictures and text together make a stronger presentation that gets the point across to different types of learners.

Share Yourself

Sharing yourself is another way to aid communication and build connections on the web. By sharing, though, I don't necessarily mean sharing intimate details about your personal life. Consider Gary Vaynerchuk's Wine Library TV and Daily Grape video blogs (at tv.winelibrary.com and www.dailygrape.com), as an example. (As of August 2011, Gary stopped producing wine-related videos. He still regularly creates and posts video content at www.gary vaynerchuk.com.) While he did occasionally share personal details, like his love of a certain football team or the birth of his baby, for the most part he wasn't sharing intimate details about his family or his personal viewpoints on politics. Instead, he shared his passion—in Gary's case, his passion about wine. He also shared some personal quirks in how he speaks; his personality came out through his writing. Primarily, he shared his expertise, which is unique to him.

Watching Gary share his passion helped viewers and readers connect with him and feel like they know him, even if just a little bit. It made him more authentic and helped provide that face2face human connection.

One easy way to share yourself is to share your opinion or share your perspective on an event or service (or new product). For instance, say you own a small business that makes cupcakes. Well, why not tell people why you like your new cupcake creation? Tell them which one of your cupcakes is your favorite (and why). Share why you decided to use certain ingredients or why your ingredients are special.

Sharing your passion about something spreads your enthusiasm to others. But don't get too personal: Only share what's comfortable and appropriate. Remember, this isn't a personal blog we're talking about. We're talking about communicating with your customers as an organization or small business. Try to find the middle ground between the extremes. One extreme is sharing nothing. Instead of showing any hint of the personal, some businesses extract all casual language and turn posts into a form of bland "marketing speak." The other extreme is treating an organizational blog like a personal blog. Unless it affected or affects your business, most of your customers really don't want to hear about your recent surgery.

Find that happy medium, and start sharing ... and connecting.

Invite People to Respond

Part of the communication process includes your initiative in starting the conversation. How do you get your customers—the other side of that conversation—to do their part? The best way, honestly, is to simply ask for it. Invite your customers to comment on your blog posts. Invite them to disagree. Invite them to subscribe or to ask questions.

Here are some how-to's for communicating via blogs. Start with a few basics:

1. *Ask questions.* At the end of each blog post, ask a question. This could be a simple "What do you think?" Or it could be more detailed, like, "That's my favorite tool. What's yours and why?" People like joining in. It helps people jump into the conversation if you direct them a little bit.

2. *Leave room to respond.* Don't finish your ideas. Blogs are great for this. Many people create the beginnings of an idea in a blog post, then ask people to continue (and develop) that idea. This leaves room for commenters to add something.

3. *Use "you" a lot.* Using personal language like "you" or "me" can help draw people into the conversation because

as they're reading, your post actually reads more like a conversation.

4. *Write like you're writing to your best friend.* This can help if you're having trouble figuring out how to remove that formal, stilted "professional" language from your blog posts. I'm guessing that you don't use that formal language when writing to your mom or to a friend. Adapt some of that Facebook status update language to your blog posts, and your posts will be more approachable.

5. *Read your posts out loud as you're typing.* This is a great trick to making your posts sound more like normal spoken conversations. Simply read the post out loud. Does it sound like something you'd actually say? If not, rewrite it until it does.

6. *Invite people to visit your physical organization.* Invite readers to come to meet you. Tell them about this week's special deal. Do it "personally," via a blog post, and you just might receive some great responses (and some great business traffic, too).

Communicating via Social Networks

So far, I've focused on communicating via blogs, because they're a great example of how communication on the web works. Now let's take a peek at social networks and see how communicating as an organization works in those settings. In this instance, when I refer to social networks, I mean sites like Facebook or Twitter. We'll focus on Flickr and YouTube later on.

Everything you've already read about blogs also applies to social networks. But there are some differences, too. One big difference is the medium: Conversations in social networks are usually shorter, and there are usually more of them. These conversations are generally even more casual than a comment on a blog post. If blogging is business casual, then social networks are more "weekend casual." Think of these more like conversations taking place at a popular dance club. Lots of different conversations are taking place, and it's easy to flit from one to the other to find something interesting. This makes social network conversations easier to start, and it's easier to jump in and out.

There are many ways to participate on social networks:

- Status updates: Most social networks have a way to post a small chunk of text. That's pretty much all that happens on Twitter—typing 140 characters and hitting the Tweet button to publish. Facebook's status updates serve a similar function, as do parts of Foursquare and LinkedIn. These text box status updates are a fun way to share what's on your mind or what you're doing—or as an organization, what's going on, what's new, and what's coming soon.

- Commenting on status updates: In Twitter, this is called a mention; in Facebook, it simply involves leaving a comment underneath a status update. Either way, commenting allows you to start conversations. As an organization, this is mighty powerful. You can ask a question and quickly get responses.

- Sharing stuff: Many social networks allow sharing. Links, pictures, or videos are popular things to share. As an organization, you can share relevant news stories, pictures of a new product, videos of a new service, etc. Then you can follow up by asking "What do you think?" or "Come see it tomorrow at the grand opening!"

- Browsing for information on a profile page: Most social networks include a profile page that describes a little about the individual or business. The profile page is handy for two reasons: 1) For customers who talk to you a lot, you can find out if they live in the area and what they like—and maybe offer them a special or remind them of a service you have that they'd be interested in, and 2) you can share important information about your organization or business. Your profile page should include hours of operation, locations, a map, your address, links to your main website for more information, and a brief description of what it is you do—for starters. Fill your customers in, so they don't have to click all over the place to find out about you. Make this easy for them.

- Liking something: This can be a Like on Facebook or a favorite on Twitter. Five-star rating systems are also a way of showing relative likes or dislikes. Liking is a way to show, well, that you liked something. Sometimes those Likes can be shared with others who follow your social stream.

- Checking in: Location-based services like Foursquare or location-sharing tools in Facebook and Google+ allow you to check in to a place. This capability basically tells the world where you are and what you're doing at any given time. Your company should create profiles in these location-based social networks. Let customers check in—and give them an incentive to do so. Give the "mayor" of a place (the person who has checked in most often on Foursquare) a 10 percent discount or offer a free cup of coffee to everyone who checks in next Wednesday. Give them a reason to keep visiting.

"Being There"

This may sound weird, but you have to actually "be there" to participate. Digitally, this means that you have to have an account set up, have a profile filled out, and—more importantly—you have to actually do the "stuff" of the social network.

So, using Facebook as an example, you need to post regular status updates. You need to post links to websites or pictures of what's happening at your business—maybe even a video of the store owner explaining a new service. You need to be there, answering questions, thanking people for comments, and inviting them into the store. Doing these types of things in social networks assures your customers that there's a real person at the other end—instead of empty cyberspace. Participating makes you "real" and "alive" within that social network.

Friending

Friending creates an immediate social connection and is another way to "be there" on social networks. Once you're connected, if a friend posts a status update or a picture, you'll get an alert. Friending is simple: In most cases, you just click the Friend link. Your goal is to have customers friend you, and that takes some initiative on their part. They need to visit your social network profile, poke around a bit, and decide you are friend-worthy. Or they may just Like your status update and friend you on a whim.

Friending also takes interaction, since customers have to see something and respond. It also takes a bit of trust. People friend you because they want that connection to you and your organization. Customers gain something by friending you, too. In some cases, they might get more information from you than if they weren't your friends, since some social networks give more access to friends.

Friending also provides a direct way to contact you. For example, in Twitter, you can only direct message someone if you both have friended each other.

What This Means for an Organization

Communication (and the connections that occur from that communication) on social networks is a great way to connect with your community. This assumes that you actually want a community of users, which is not really a radical idea. At some level, you probably already have a physical community of regular customers. Online, you probably already have a community of sorts, too. People are probably already talking about you online. Why not join in the conversation?

When customers friend and hold conversations with your organization, it makes you that much more human to your customers. Suddenly, Sally in Marketing becomes the "voice of the organization." The organization is communicating and interacting. When you implement these ideas as an organization, you share your organizational identity with your customers. And that's the goal, isn't it? Organizationally, you want people thinking face2face about your organization—feeling a personal connection to your organization or business.

If you have vibrant online communications, your customers get satisfaction from the "relationship" they have with the organization. That's a pretty good start to building and solidifying customer relations.

Endnotes

1. Chris Brogan, "11 Free Resources About Creativity," Chris Brogan (blog), January 7, 2011, accessed March 18, 2012, www.chrisbrogan.com/11-creativity-resources.

2. David Lee King, "Am I a 2.0 Librarian and the Library 2.0 Spectrum," David Lee King (blog), August 1, 2007, accessed January 18, 2012, www.davidleeking.com/2007/08/01/am-i-a-20-librarian-and-the-library-20-spectrum.

3. "Statement of Rights and Responsibilities," Facebook, last modified April 26, 2011, accessed January 18, 2012, www.facebook.com/legal/terms.

4. "Flickr Community Guidelines," Flickr, accessed January 18, 2012, www.flickr.com/guidelines.gne.

5. "Community Discussion Guidelines," Topeka & Shawnee County Public Library, accessed January 18, 2012, tscpl.org/about/policies/community discussion-guidelines. Adapted from Flickr's Community Guidelines (www.flickr.com/guidelines.gne), Facebook's Statement of Rights and Responsibilities (www.facebook.com/legal/terms), and Patrick O'Keefe's User Guidelines, found at www.managingonlineforums.com/downloadable-templates.

6. David Lee King, "Rethinking the 3rd Place," David Lee King (blog), September 22, 2009, accessed January 18, 2012, www.davidleeking.com/2009/09/22/rethinking-the-3rd-place.

7. David Lee King, "10 Tips to Do Presentations Like Me: Use Presenter View," David Lee King (blog), January 13, 2011, accessed January 18, 2012, www.davidleeking.com/2011/01/13/10-tips-to-do-presentations-like-me-use-presenter-view.

8. Darren Rowse, "Using Photos in Your Posts," ProBlogger, April 20, 2005, accessed January 18, 2012, www.problogger.net/archives/2005/04/20/using-photos-in-your-posts.

CHAPTER 3

Face2Face With Cameras and Video

Up until now, we've been exploring primarily text-based ways to communicate with customers. Using tools like blogs or status updates lets your voice be heard and lets you "be seen" online. Now, let's get a little more advanced.

In many ways, the digital world does mirror what goes on in the physical, "real" world. For example, "being seen" physically for your business might mean attending an event such as a Chamber of Commerce meet-and-greet. These types of events give you the opportunity to meet people, to share thoughts or ideas, and to exchange business cards. These events also have what I call the "Romper Room" effect. Remember that old kids' TV show? At the end of each show, the hostess looked through a "magic mirror" and would name children she "saw" watching the show, saying something like "I can see David, and Judy, and Nathan!" Over time, you start to recognize the people who attend the same events that you do.

The same thing happens online. For example, over time I have started to recognize the people I "hang out" with on Twitter. I recognize their Twitter icons (an image that represents their site, usually a small photograph of the person). I will "see them" online when they are active on Twitter.

Social media sometimes also connects the digital back to the physical. For example, while writing this book, I would spend time in Starbucks working on edits. While I was getting my Starbucks drink, I "checked in" using Foursquare. Later on, one of my friends did the same thing—got a drink at the same Starbucks and checked in ... and noticed I was here. That's one thing Foursquare does: It lets you know if your friends are in the same place. So he came over and said hi, all because of that mutual check-in.

This chapter explores how you can use images and videos as visual tools to connect with your customers. You will also find tips about how to most effectively use pictures and videos organizationally.

Face2Face via Pictures

Pictures can help your organization connect with customers. I use Flickr pretty heavily and love posting "what's going on in my life" photos. I often use Flickr to show what's happening in my day—sharing pictures of a new hat, pictures out of my hotel window, or even pictures of myself.

Guess what? Because I share pictures of myself, people tend to recognize me when I speak at information industry conferences and meetings. This has come in handy at times, like when someone I had never met in person recently had to pick me up at the airport. The person had visited my Flickr photos account, seen my pictures, and recognized me easily.

David Armano, executive vice president at Global Innovation and Integration for Edelman Digital and blogger at Logic + Emotion (www.darmano.typepad.com), has used pictures to raise money for a family.[1] In 2009, a single mom he knew was having a rough time making ends meet. Daniela was a Romanian immigrant, couldn't speak much English, and had just gone through a divorce. David and his family decided to help out a friend in need.

On a whim, David decided to post Daniela's story and asked his blog readers to help him raise $5,000 to help her out. David writes well, so the story was compelling. But he also took a photo of Daniela and her kids—and that was even more compelling. Within a day or so, David had raised more than $5,000 ... he actually raised $16,880.60! His goal was furthered by a photograph that helped readers visually connect with the plight of Daniela's family.

How about pictures or photographs that don't include people—do they make a difference? Well, have you ever used Google Maps Street View to visually figure out where you're going? I sure have. I use it to scout out landmarks when I'm headed somewhere unfamiliar, because it lets me "visit" and see where I'm supposed to be before I'm supposed to be there. Pictures can help emphasize events. For example, many people used Google Maps to check out the damage in Port au Prince after the Haiti earthquake. Those satellite images let viewers see the seriousness of the damage and helped compel people to donate time and money to assist with the cleanup efforts.

Photographs have become much easier to deal with in the last 10–20 years. No more film or processing to mess with (unless you choose to do that). Since photo files are born digital, you don't have to scan or otherwise convert them into a usable digital format. You don't even have to carry a full-fledged camera around anymore—my iPhone camera takes photos that are similar in quality to my old snapshot 110 film camera. Since I always have my iPhone with me, I can take a snapshot whenever I want.

Uploading photographs to the web is also extremely simple. Two popular destinations for photos, Flickr and Facebook, make it very easy to upload and add photographs to your social network pages. Many mobile-based social apps allow you to upload a photograph directly from the app to the online photo service, which makes the upload process even easier. Just press "upload," and you're done. Figure 3.1 shows how to upload images to Facebook.

Figure 3.1   Uploading images in Facebook

Permissions and Photographers' Rights

Before we dive any deeper into using photos and videos, let's talk about permissions. Do you, as an organization, need permission to take photos or videos of people, to post them, and to use them as part of your business? The easy answer is ... there is no easy answer. Here's what I mean.

No Permission Needed

Sometimes, permission is not needed. If you live in the U.S., you have the right to take photographs and videos of anyone and anything in a public place (with some restrictions). But don't take my word for that—check out these resources:

- From the American Civil Liberties Union: "When in public spaces where you are lawfully present you have the right to photograph anything that is in plain view. That includes pictures of federal buildings, transportation facilities, and police. Such photography is a form of public oversight over the government and is important in a free society."[2]

- From Photojojo.com: "Anyone in a public place can take pictures of anything they want. Public places include parks, sidewalks, malls, etc. Malls? Yeah. Even though it's technically private property, being open to the public makes it public space."[3]

- From *The Photographer's Right: Your Rights and Remedies When Stopped or Confronted for Photography*, by Bert P. Krages II, an attorney who concentrates on intellectual property and environmental law: "The general rule in the United States is that anyone may take photographs of whatever they want when they are in a public place or places where they have permission to take photographs.

> Absent a specific legal prohibition such as a statute or
> ordinance, you are legally entitled to take photographs.
> Examples of places that are traditionally considered
> public are streets, sidewalks, and public parks."[4]

Permission Needed

Sometimes, permission is needed. Here's what Andrew Kantor, a technology writer for *USA TODAY*, says about the commercial use of photography:

> You can't put someone else's likeness to commercial use
> without their permission. This is usually mentioned in
> terms of celebrities, but it applies to making money from
> anyone's likeness. ... For example, if you shoot individ-
> ual kids playing in a school football game, you can't try to
> sell those shots to the parents; the kids have a right to the
> use of their likeness. You can sell photos of the game in
> general, though, and any shots where what's happening
> ("A player celebrates a goal") is more important than
> who's doing it ("Star running back John Doe takes a
> momentary rest"). Sound like a gray area? It is if you're
> planning to sell the pictures but not if you're simply dis-
> playing them. And if you're using them for news pur-
> poses, all bets are off—you can pretty much publish
> whatever you want if it happens in public view."[5]

See why I said there is no easy answer? We haven't even discussed social media yet. Social media is primarily used for communication or to simply share "what's happening"—the "news" of
your organization. If that's how you primarily use photos and
videos online, you are probably good to go. If you plan on using
those images (and specific likenesses of individuals) for commercial purposes, then you need a permissions form.

Also remember this: I'm no attorney. If you have access to an attorney, and you or your organization is concerned about organizational use of photos and videos, please consult with him or her. Attorneys don't like surprises!

Where to Share Pictures

You can share pictures many places online, but only a few really matter to organizations. Let's discuss each of these, and then I'll provide some how-to's for handling pictures and photographs as an organization.

Blogs

You can share pictures on your organization's blog. I mentioned this in the previous chapter, but it's worth repeating: Photographs make your blog seem more friendly and approachable. For example, you could feature staff members on your blog. Provide their names, share their pictures, and give a little bit of information about them, such as their favorite books, favorite ice cream flavors, and why they like working at your organization. Your staff member, and therefore the organization, now has a name and a face. You have just personalized your organization, making it more human and approachable to customers. Now, when customers who visited that blog post think of your organization, they might think of that person. That's a good thing—it means your customer has internalized what your organization looks like to them.

Photographs can also add to or enhance content. On my personal blog, I frequently use images to visually enhance my blog posts. For example, a PR firm let me drive a Ford Flex for a week with the understanding that I would blog about my experience. I took photos of various features of the car and used those photos to enhance my posts (Figure 3.2).

Flickr

Organizations can use Flickr to share what they're doing. Have a new product or service? Give customers a "sneak peek" before that product hits the shelves. Since people search for photos in Flickr, you'll want to use plenty of relevant tags on each photo. A tag is a word or words used to describe something, which can be attached to images in Flickr. For example, if I took a photo of Starbucks, I might describe the photo with these tags: *starbucks*, *coffee*, and

Figure 3.2   My Ford Flex post

caffeine. Also, use descriptive titles on each photo, since the title field is searchable.

Of course, people can also comment on Flickr photos (if you've allowed comments in your Flickr account). Commenting on photos allows customers to ask questions about what they're seeing. And you can answer them easily via the comment box.

Facebook

Your organization's Facebook Page acts very similarly to a personal Facebook profile, complete with a Photos section. So, upload those photos! They'll appear on your Facebook Wall in the status updates section, so people can comment on them. You can also set up your Flickr feed to automatically dump photos to your Facebook Wall by connecting your Flickr and Facebook accounts (more information on that can be found at Flickr). There are also third-party tools that will automatically import Flickr photos to your Facebook photos page.

Twitter

Twitter resembles the status update feature of Facebook. In fact, that's all it does! Twitter lets you tell your story, and using pictures with Twitter helps to visually tell that story.

There are a variety of ways to share photos in Twitter, including Twitter's own upload service (which hosts photos on Photobucket). You can point to URLs, such as the address of a Flickr photo. (Twitter might shorten the URL for you, so you can get more text into that 140-character text box.) You can also use a third-party tool to post pictures to Twitter. For example, I use Twitpic, which uploads a photo to www.twitpic.com and also posts it to Twitter with a shortened Twitpic URL. TweetDeck (www.tweetdeck.com), which is the Twitter reader I most often use, includes a photo viewer within the app, so I don't have to click a link and visit a website to view the image.

How to Use Pictures Organizationally

The following are some ideas on how to use photos in an organizational setting.

Use Pictures of Staff

When you feature staff members, use pictures of the employees who actually interact in those spaces. For example, if Marlene is your primary blogger, include a picture of her once in awhile, so your blog readers can put a face to the "voice." Make sure these are nice-quality images, but no glamour shots needed! Make sure the photos are recent photos, too. If the photo is more than 5 years old, you most likely need a new one.

Photos should also be business casual. No beers in hand (unless you're a bar). No slouching, T-shirt-wearing, "yeah, it's the weekend" pictures. You most likely have some dress standards at work, and some professional standards in your business for staff. The same guidelines would apply for photographs of your staff used online.

Use Pictures to Be Helpful

You can show useful, helpful things about your business using a photograph. For example, if something major in your store or company has changed—for example, a new entrance or a new branch—you can show it in advance, using pictures posted to your website and to Facebook. This prepares your digitally savvy customers for the change—before they actually visit your business.

Be Pleasant

You should have a real smile on your face in your pictures. If you look surly or unapproachable, the impression transfers to your business. This especially holds true in a very social place like Facebook. Who wants to friend "Mr. Grumpy"?

Choose the Right Photo Angle

When taking photos of your staff, try to position them so they're doing one of two things:

1. Looking at the camera: A person looking directly at the camera seems to be looking at the viewer. If you add that photo to your organization's website, the employee is looking at customers, maintaining eye contact—just like in a physical conversation. My Facebook profile picture uses this strategy (Figure 3.3).

Figure 3.3   Looking at YOU on my Facebook profile

2. "Looking" at your content: When adding a photo to content, position it so the photo leads the person visually to the content. So, if there's an angle in the photo, make the angle lean toward the content, rather than away from it. The same holds true for people shots. If you add a photo to a blog post of a person looking to the right or left, position the picture so the person is looking at the content and not away from it. Looking away from the content makes the person in the picture look aloof and disinterested. It's a small detail, but it is noticeable.

Focus on the Face

When taking pictures of staff, especially pictures that might be used as an icon/avatar picture for Facebook or Twitter, get a headshot—one as closely cropped as possible.

Why? Those icon pictures are tiny! Even a head-and-shoulders shot, when small, hides what the person looks like. This can distract from the friendliness of the image (and, therefore, the friendliness of the website itself).

Some Do's and Don'ts

Here are a few more do's and don't of using photos:

Don't hide.

Don't do a faraway shot or a shot of you hiding partially behind a book. Yes, they're cute. Yes, they're artsy. But they also hide who you are, and that's not the goal. You don't want your organization to seem like it's hiding from customers.

Do represent your company. Be professional; be friendly in your picture. Try to look as approachable as possible. Practice this if needed. Spend some time taking photos of yourself so you get used to it.

Face2Face via Videos

I enjoy playing guitar and love watching the videos created by ProGuitarShop, a guitar store in the Portland, Oregon area (www.proguitarshop.com). ProGuitarShop has a YouTube channel (www.youtube.com/user/ProGuitarShopDemos) that features one of its employees testing out new guitar equipment (guitars, guitar amps, and guitar effects pedals). The videos are done well, they give the viewer just enough information to know more about the product being tested, and handy links are provided to ProGuitarShop's website (in hopes that you actually buy the product being tested).

What is ProGuitarShop doing with video? It is introducing customers, via video, to its inventory, to its staff (and the way they play guitar), and to the company's goal of being "a premier online and local retailer for your guitar needs."[6]

Ways to Use Videos Organizationally

In what ways can you use a video to add the human dimension and help you create face2face connections?

Share Yourself

Just like ProGuitarShop, when you share something via a video, you are sharing a little part of yourself and your organization. Your body language and movements, how you phrase things, even some of your mannerisms might come through.

Share Your Thoughts

When you make a video, you're sharing your thoughts. You are telling us what you find important. When you share via a video, you will probably give a bit more thought to the message and to details like what you're wearing. So, you have more opportunity to craft your thoughts and emphasize particular points.

Your well-planned message—consisting of your idea, plus your passion, plus your unique body language and facial expressions—helps drive your point home.

Remember Format Familiarity

These days, most of your customers are used to connecting to people, ideas, and stories through video. Don't believe me? Answer this: Have you ever cried while watching a movie or been moved by a dramatic turn in the plot?

I'm guessing your answer was yes. Some of us are even moved occasionally while watching the evening news when a powerful story is being told. My point? We are used to connecting through video. It's really not a new format at all. So using video to share your organization's story, or the story of what you sell or make as a business, can be a powerful tool for current and future customers.

Introduce People

Of course you can use video to introduce a new product. But why not use video to introduce your customers to other people? With video, you can do things like interview key clients and share their part of your story—how they use your services or products. Or look internally and introduce your customers to a new staff member.

This connection you show between you and the other person on the video helps demonstrate to your customers and viewers how you would interact with them as well.

How to Use Video to Connect

We have just learned how video helps connect you to your customers and how it helps your organization seem more human. Now let's talk about some how-to's for video. These how-to's, for the most part, have nothing to do with the mechanics of creating video—nothing about formats or specific cameras or proper lighting techniques. Other books (start with Steve Garfield's *Get Seen: Online Video Secrets to Building Your Business*[7]) do a great job with the specifics of video on the web.

Honestly, the camera isn't the most important ingredient. You can create a video that successfully connects you to customers by using the webcam built in to your laptop or by using a cheap webcam. And you can create a terrible video with a $5,000-plus professional video camera. Focus on connecting to customers, and upgrade your camera when you start to "outgrow" your current setup. That time will look different for everyone ... and you will know when it happens!

Here are some general pointers that will help your videos stand out from the pack.

Be Informal

Remove formal language in your videos. The more formal you are, the less real you seem, especially in a video. So keep it informal. One way to do that is not to script what you're going to say.

Does this sound difficult? I confess, I'm not a person who does well unscripted. If I didn't script myself, at least somewhat, I'd talk for twice as long, or twice as short, and say half as much! Sometimes, I will completely script my videos with line-by-line phrases. Other times, I'll create an outline of what I want to say beforehand. Then, during video creation, I will give those ideas in my outline my best shot. I wing each section while following the roadmap of my outline.

While you're speaking in that casual tone, relax! Some of us feel uncomfortable when a camera is pointing at us. We might start overthinking our words and generally just don't act like ourselves.

How do you get over that self-conscious feeling? The only way I know is to practice, practice, practice. Make lots of videos of you talking—sharing something, even if it's just a hobby you enjoy. Do anything you can to get used to talking to a tiny lens pointed at your head.

Your comfort level shows—a lot—on a video. If you are uncomfortable talking about a product or service on a video, that will show. It will make it look like you are uncomfortable with that product, and you don't want that. So practice in front of the video camera.

Keep It Short

Some of us are talkers. We *love* to talk. We love to share the tiniest details. But with video, especially with web-based video, the goal is to keep the video as short as possible. Your goal is to create videos that are 2 minutes or less in length. To do this, only share one or two ideas per video. If your idea is still too long, make a multipart series of videos to cover the whole topic. End the first video with, "Watch next week for the second part." That might keep your customers watching.

Some Handy Video Tricks

The following are some lessons I've learned while making videos that you can use, too.

Talk to the Camera Lens

When creating a video where you're talking to your audience, talk to the camera lens. It feels weird—especially if there are other people in the room. But when you look at and talk to the camera lens, you will appear in your video to be looking at and talking to your customers.

Edit Your Videos

Be sure to edit out extraneous material. There are probably sentences you don't really need. Also, cut out any huge pauses or those "ahs" and "ums" you might have said. They're not needed and add up time-wise.

Talk Toward the Light

Always face the light. You want people to see you. If you're outside, face toward the sun and point your camera away from the sun. Inside, if you don't have studio lights of some sort, find a bright window and face it.

Shoot More Than You Need

You need more video than you think. So, shoot lots of video, even if your final video will only be 2 minutes long. If you're talking about a product your business sells or a service your organization offers, shoot some B-Roll—video showing that product or service, without you actually talking. When the main narrative or story is playing in the video, you can insert your B-Roll video over your narrative to break up the video a bit and make it more interesting.

Also, leave extra space at the beginning and the end of each video clip you create. You generally need extra space for edits and for fading in and out. Add 10 seconds before and after each video clip you create. You'll be very glad you did when you edit.

Helping Your Organization Be More Human

How do videos help your organization be more human and help you connect your organization to your customers? Videos:

- Show off your staff: Showing off a staff member in a positive way makes the whole organization that much more human. While photos provide a human face to the organization, videos take that idea one step further, because viewers not only hear the person, they also see him.

- Show off your organization: Connections also happen through your video content. Your customers already like watching videos—on TV, at the movies, and probably even on the web. If you are using video to show off the details of your organization, you are using a format that is already popular with a large and growing segment of your customers. So, use video to show off your organization and staff, your building, your services, your products, or the departments that help create these services.

- Show off your customers: Seeing actual customers using a service makes that service seem that much more usable to people.

Photos, Videos, and Organizations

Videos and photos are great tools to connect in a visual way with your customers. They lend a sense of familiarity to your organization and to your products and services—maybe even to your staff and some of your customers, too.

Watching a video or seeing some pictures makes "you," in the organizational sense, seem so much friendlier and more familiar. Videos and photos help make the not too familiar … much more familiar. Therefore they bridge the gap, making the face2face happen much more easily.

Endnotes

1. David Armano, "Please Help Us Help Daniela's Family," Logic + Emotion (blog), January 6, 2009, accessed January 19, 2012, www.darmano.typepad.com/logic_emotion/2009/01/pleas-help-us-help-daniellas-family.html.

2. American Civil Liberties Union, "Know Your Rights: Photographers,"
    ACLU.org, accessed April 10, 2012, www.aclu.org/free-speech/know-your-
    rights-photographers.

3. "Photography and The Law: Know Your Rights," Photojojo.com, March 17,
    2008, accessed April 10, 2012, content.photojojo.com/tips/legal-rights-of-
    photographers.

4. Bert P. Krages II, *The Photographer's Right: Your Rights and Remedies When
    Stopped or Confronted for Photography*, accessed April 10, 2012, www.krages.
    com/ThePhotographersRight.pdf.

5. Andrew Kantor, "Misinformation About Your Photography Rights Continues to
    Spread," USAToday.com, August 11, 2006, accessed April 10, 2012, www.usa
    today.com/tech/columnist/andrewkantor/2006-08-11-photography-
    rights_x.htm.

6. "ProGuitarShop Collective," Facebook, accessed April 10, 2012, www.face
    book.com/ProGuitarShopPage.

7. Steve Garfield, *Get Seen: Online Video Secrets to Building Your Business* (New
    York: John Wiley & Sons, 2010).

CHAPTER
4

Community Connections

Ever heard of a grassroots online community that formed around a product, service, organization, or an idea? In this chapter, I'll explain how these types of communities form, share some handy tools that can be used to help support these online communities, and, in the process, provide some ways your organization can have a human touch while interacting with customers in these community-driven spaces.

One grassroots community project was Think Big Topeka. In 2010, a group of entrepreneurs in Topeka had heard about Google's interesting fiber experiment. Here's what Google said it wanted to do: "Google is planning to build and test ultra-high speed broadband networks in a small number of trial locations across the country. We'll deliver internet speeds more than 100 times faster than what most Americans have access to today with 1 gigabit per second, fiber-to-the-home connections. We'll offer service at a competitive price to at least 50,000, and potentially up to 500,000 people."[1]

Pretty cool project! That's what the entrepreneurs in Topeka thought. So they created a Facebook group called Think Big Topeka and started rallying their group of friends. The Facebook group quickly grew (as of July 2011, the group had 16,678 members). The members of the group also created a more traditional website to get their message out and started talking about the project to anyone who would listen.

They didn't just share in the traditional "let's set up a meeting" way. They also staged some flash mobs at events to get local recognition, created videos for YouTube, and talked to the city council and the mayor of Topeka. The mayor liked the idea enough that the city filled out the necessary paperwork, and the mayor declared that, for the month of March, Topeka would be renamed Google, Kansas. That got some media attention. CNN, the *New York Times*, and other traditional news sources noticed and ran the AP article. Popular online news organizations like TechCrunch, the Huffington Post, and Mashable also ran articles.

On April 1, 2010, Google even played along. Google usually does something funny for April Fools' Day, so that year, Google decided to change its name from Google to Topeka (Figure 4.1)—complete with a touched-up image of the sign outside Google's building.[2]

Topeka ultimately didn't land the Google fiber project—Kansas City, Kansas, did—which is about 75 miles from Topeka. But Topeka was the only city that prompted Google to change its name for a day!

This project gave Topekans something to rally behind, and that initial grassroots effort has spilled over into other local community groups. Now there are multiple community groups in Topeka focused on making Topeka better. For example, there's a downtown revitalization project that hadn't seen the light of day in previous incarnations. This time, the project has the support of younger professionals who had already learned to band together

Figure 4.1   Google's name change on April Fool's Day 2010

from the Think Big Topeka project, and the momentum for revitalization is growing.

What happened here? There was a lot of connection, online and offline. Traditional meetings, social functions, and even things like the flash mobs were scheduled. But there were also face2face online connections happening on the website, the blog, and the Facebook group and Page. Connections also happened on Twitter through an account and multiple hashtags. A hashtag is a simple way to add tags or keywords to tweets. Once added, you can subscribe to that hashtag and follow the conversation via the hashtag. To create a Twitter hashtag, add the "#" character before a word in your tweet, such as *#topeka*. This turns the word into a hashtag. People wanted to see Google's fiber project come to Topeka. But, even more than that, they wanted their sleepy town to start taking responsibility for its future.

Not bad for a bunch of young professionals and a Facebook group.

Meet People and Make Community Connections

Getting communities moving toward an action takes a lot of effort. It takes getting out and meeting people, but not just in traditional meetings and in-person social gatherings. Online meetings can also take place.

I work with the American Library Association (ALA), a nonprofit association that supports libraries and librarians, by serving on a variety of committees and task forces. We do traditional-type work, with task groups and committees, but we accomplish much of it online. We use tools like email or Skype to hold meetings, and we use wiki software or Google Docs to write our reports or other materials we need to support our projects. Everyone can participate by sharing thoughts and editing the documentation.

I have yet to meet some of my ALA colleagues in person. But we have met and accomplished real work together, online.

When you think about online meetings in regard to making face2face community connections, there are three important concepts: sharing a commonality, meeting your customers, and doing actual work. Let's unpack each of those a bit.

Sharing a Commonality

Have you ever read about your favorite hobby or pastime online, and then discovered a group of people gathered around that pastime in an online forum? I certainly have. I have participated in forums focused on a particular type of electric guitar (insert a big shout out to Telecaster players—w00t!). My brother-in-law frequents a forum for church music leaders and musicians, where participants can share ideas and give suggestions to others for their worship services.

Is knitting your thing? Check out Ravelry (www.ravelry.com). "Ravelry is a place for knitters, crocheters, designers, spinners, weavers and dyers to keep track of their yarn, tools, project and pattern information, and look to others for ideas and inspiration. The content here is all user-driven; we as a community make the site what it is. Ravelry is a great place for you to keep notes about your projects, see what other people are making, find the perfect pattern and connect with people who love to play with yarn from all over the world in our forums."[3] Ravelry also has a Facebook Page followed by over 93,000 people and a Twitter account followed by more than 25,000 people. That's a lot of well-connected knitters!

Online community can work in the same way for organizations and businesses. Most organizations and businesses have a central goal or mission, or a product or service they create for their customers. Similar organizations tend to form like-minded communities around those goals already. ALA is one example. Online, ALA has created ALA Connect—a community-based website where committees and groups of librarians can work through current issues and problems facing libraries, or do their committee work for the organization.

Many small businesses use tools like Basecamp (www.basecamp hq.com) for online collaboration and project planning. Basecamp is an online service that facilitates project planning and collaboration by providing areas for communication and comments, for sharing files connected to the project, and for assigning due dates to project timelines.

Meeting Your Customers

It's important to have multiple ways for your customers to connect with you as an organization. I have already mentioned social networks and blogs. Now, let's consider traditional meeting formats, but with a twist. Tweetups are one example. A tweetup is a meeting of local Twitter users who get together for primarily social reasons—to network or to simply to meet the people they talk to on

Twitter in person. Meeting in-person helps solidify those online discussions and put a face to the people you talk to on Twitter.

Local conferences are another great way to meet in-person. One way social media lovers in Topeka do this is through Podcamp Topeka. Podcamp Topeka is a regional unconference our library created to serve our social media community. We've held this podcamp-styled unconference for 3 years now, and in 2011, we attracted more than 100 people—for the most part locals, although we had people from five states participate. This event gives people a chance to share what they do, to ask questions, and to network with each other in-person.

Doing Actual Work

I mentioned doing library association work in online settings. But how about what Patrick O'Keefe does? He runs the iFroggy Network, a "network of content, community and ecommerce sites covering various interests."[4] This includes forums, which have moderators. But Patrick has never actually met many of these moderators in person. Instead, he manages them over the web.

Patrick was the keynote speaker at Podcamp Topeka 2010. One of his forum moderators lives in Kansas and decided to come to the event, and he and Patrick met for the first time in-person—although they had already been doing real work together, and they'd already met online. Here's what Patrick said about that meeting:

> As a community related aside, a longtime staff member and moderator on KarateForums.com, one of the communities that I manage, drove 3 hours from Hays, Kansas, to be at the event so that we could meet for the first time. His name is Brian Walker and it was great to be able to meet him and his family in person and chat. I even brought him in on a breakout session I led,

"Moderating an Online Forum," where we talked about how we do things at KarateForums.com. It was great.[5]

The combination of actual face-to-face meetings and online face2face interactions can be a powerful combination.

Make Twitter, Facebook, and Community Connections

Now let's look at a few ways Twitter and Facebook can help organizations create face2face connections with their customers. Tweets and status updates can certainly make the difference between a very passive organization and a vibrant, active one. For example, in the 2010–2011 Tunisia revolution, social media was used in at least four ways, all of which can be applied in these other contexts:

1. To engage in grassroots mobilization: Some of the organization of the protests happened on Facebook, which served as a community organizing platform for the protests.

2. To organize the rise of civil society and active citizenship: Citizens used social media to identify the positions of snipers, police, and looters, and to alert one another to violence. Networks also formed to clean streets, protect shops, and organize food lines.

3. To counter rumors or propaganda: When there were concerns about water being poisoned, people shared information on Facebook to help to counter those rumors. When reports came in that there was a massive shooting in a neighborhood, they were debunked by a number of people.

4. To help people analyze government statements: When the government went on TV to make a statement, people went online to analyze what the political leaders said and to form a consensus on whether the positions met their requirements.

Would the revolution have happened without social media? Yes, but it probably would not have happened as fast.[6]

Or, remember the story of the Berkeley graduate journalism student James Karl Buck who was jailed in Egypt? He was taking photos of a demonstration and was arrested. No one confiscated his phone, so he quickly tweeted "Arrested" (Figure 4.2)—and his Twitter followers started making calls. They were able to reach the U.S. Embassy and Buck's college, among other places. Because of his tweets, Buck's college hired a lawyer on Buck's behalf, and Buck was released.[7]

Twitter is actually quite good at relaying breaking news. There are a growing number of reporters and interested Twitter users who share important-sounding events on Twitter as those events

Figure 4.2   James Karl Buck's famous tweet that mobilized his followers

are happening. I've even seen this locally. Kansas is part of tornado alley. In the springtime, when the weather gets nasty, I can follow what's happening by checking in with local Twitter users. The local news even tweets minute-by-minute updates about tornado warnings, including where a tornado is headed, and shares damage reports from other Twitter users.

I personally use Twitter as sort of an extended think tank. If I have an interesting thought or a question related to my field, I can simply mention it in Twitter and ask for responses. Within minutes, I usually have 10–20 responses from other people sharing their opinions on my question.

Using Twitter as a think tank works great for businesses. First, follow some Twitter users who work in your industry—maybe 100 or so. Second, start to interact with this group—respond to tweets of people you follow, or answer questions you see when it makes sense to do so. Third, do you have a burning question that might help your business or organization move to the next level? Ask via a tweet. Your question will likely be answered a variety of ways.

Be Human in Status Updates

Can an organization be human in a status update? Yes, it can! There's definitely a balance here. It can be hard for an individual to share organizationally without getting too personal on an organizational account (we've all probably read about goof-ups made by people accidentally sharing personal tweets on an organizational Twitter account).

But you can still share a bit of yourself while sharing about the organization, can't you? There's a healthy balance to strike between personal and professional. Figuring out this balance actually helps the organization or business come across as human in a variety of online social settings. Here are some ideas to get you started down that path.

Share Quick Thoughts

You can share quick thoughts about your industry or services. When you do this, in effect you are sharing what's on the organization's collective mind. For example, at a library, a staff member can share information about new books as they arrive or maybe announce an upcoming author talk. If it's getting close to tax season, a blogger can share information about all the resources a library has to help people do their taxes.

It works much the same way for a nonprofit. What's on the nonprofit's mind? Share your thoughts about programs, new services provided, and—most importantly—why the new services are provided and why potential users of those services should care. Maybe there are hidden shortcuts or services that the nonprofit provides, but they are hard to navigate. Sharing this type of "insider information" helps make your customers feel like they're insiders, too.

In both cases, by sharing this type of information, you are sharing what's on the organization's collective mind. You are creating those face2face connections ... organizationally. And, in the process, it makes your organization seem more human.

Continue Conversations

We can also create and continue conversations online. If your organization has a Twitter or Facebook account, for example, your customers can ask questions—either publicly through the status update box or privately via direct messages in Twitter and messages in Facebook.

These questions can be the start of a conversation. Your organization continues those conversations by answering the questions. Zappos does this well. It uses a variety of Twitter accounts to answer questions customers might have. Here's an example of this type of interaction:

@kagrrakid said, "@Zappos_Service Thanks to upgraded shipping I got my new boots just in time for a good old Chicago blizzard. Thanks Zappos!!"[8]

Zappos Service replied back, "@kagrrakid Your welcome. Please stay safe and I hope the boots will keep you warm."[9]

How cool is that? A company that sells shoes actually cared about a customer enough to tell him or her to stay safe and keep warm.

The Nonprofit Technology Network (NTEN) is another great example of connecting with customers via Twitter. It constantly has conversations going with people.

A follower of NTEN's Twitter account asked about a text messaging tool the organization uses. NTEN replied in this way: "Hi Kate! We used @mobilecommons RT @kbladow: @NTENorg What tool do you use for text messaging evaluations at the NTC?"[10]

In both cases, Zappos and NTEN are responding quickly and accurately to their customers, which shows there's an actual person behind the organization. Doing this makes the organization much more accessible to customers and potential customers.

These two companies are also adding some nice human elements to their organizations. Interacting via Twitter or Facebook adds a conversational element to their organizations, which helps customers and website visitors feel like they are listened to. It also shows that the organization actually wants to connect with its community, simply by answering questions in an online public setting.

Just by being there, by responding, even noncustomers see that the organization is active and helpful. This is important because you want your organization to look good to potential customers—not just to the regulars who are already insiders.

More importantly, it gets your answers, information, and links to people—your customers—who need them, quickly, in their favorite spaces. It removes the logo and helps to show the person—the personality—behind the logo. And it makes your organization more human in the process.

Endnotes

1. Google, "Google Fiber for Communities: Project Overview," accessed January 23, 2012, www.google.com/appserve/fiberrfi/public/overview.

2. Google, "Google Blog: A Different Kind of Company Name," April 1, 2010, accessed January 23, 2012, www.googleblog.blogspot.com/2010/04/different-kind-of-company-name.html.

3. Ravelry, "About Us," accessed January 23, 2012, www.ravelry.com/about.

4. iFroggy Network, "Welcome," accessed January 23, 2012, www.ifroggy.com.

5. Patrick O'Keefe, "The Power of Online (Taken Offline) Community on Display at Podcamp Topeka," November 18, 2010, accessed January 23, 2012, www.managingcommunities.com/2010/11/18/the-power-of-online-taken-offline-community-on-display-at-podcamp-topeka.

6. Alex Howard, "A Tunisian on the Role of Social Media in the Revolution in Tunisia," January 30, 2011, accessed January 23, 2012, www.gov20.govfresh.com/a-tunisian-on-the-role-of-social-media-in-the-revolution-in-tunisia.

7. Mallory Simon, "Student Twitters His Way Out of Egyptian Jail," CNNTech, April 25, 2008, accessed January 23, 2012, articles.cnn.com/2008-04-25/tech/twitter.buck_1_cell-phone-blog-anti-government-protest?_s=PM:TECH.

8. Kagrrakid, Twitter post, January 31, 2011, accessed January 23, 2012, www.twitter.com/#!/kagrrakid/status/32230935655096321.

9. Zappos_Service, Twitter post, January 31, 2011, accessed January 23, 2012, www.twitter.com/#!/Zappos_Service/status/32231330603335681.

10. NTENorg, Twitter post, accessed January 23, 2012, www.twitter.com/#!/NTENorg/status/70522232224493568.

CHAPTER 5

Face2Face Listening

So far, we've learned how to talk by using blogs, photos, videos, and social networks. Now, let's learn how to listen. Listening to customers is one of the most important things an organization or business can do.

In this chapter, we'll look at what online listening entails, some ways for organizations to listen to conversations online, what to listen for, how to respond, and when to respond. Finally, we'll look at some online listening tools.

What Is Listening?

Of course we all know what listening is—we do it all the time. I listen to my wife and kids talk; they listen to me. I listen while I'm in a meeting, and other co-workers listen to me.

Online listening, though, requires an intermediate medium to get the message from the customer to the business. When organizations listen, it really means they have set up feeds that send them "mentions"—mentions of themselves, their products, or maybe pertinent keywords about their business.

Chris Brogan is a big proponent of listening as a strategy for organizations. Here's what he says about listening: "The most powerful tool in social media is listening. I say this because at the same time you're thinking about how to engage in all this new stuff, people out there are pushing commentary all over the place about what they like and don't like about your product, your competitor's product, and their needs. They're screaming out with opportunities for you to solve, and all you have to do is listen, process what you've heard, and engage with them in a reasonable way. It's the closest thing to printing money that I can tell you about."[1]

Here are some examples—some personal, some general—of online listening in action; later sections will talk about the specific tools to use.

The Author

I have a number of feeds and searches set up in Technorati, Google Blog Search, Twitter, BackType, and Topix, mainly for *davidleeking* and *david lee king*—the two versions of my name I most often find online.

Then, when someone mentions me online, that conversation, or mention, is forwarded to me. Usually, someone is quoting a blog post or magazine article that I wrote, or making a comment about a presentation I gave. Setting up these listening tools helps me see what people are saying about my thoughts and ideas, which helps me improve and learn from others.

Topeka & Shawnee County Public Library

I have created similar listening tools for my organization (Topeka & Shawnee County Public Library [TSCPL]). I have Google Blog

Searches, Twitter searches, and Topix searches set up for the more popular versions of our organization's name. That's tricky because TSCPL has such a long name. People rarely type *Topeka and Shawnee County Public Library*. So I search for that version of the name, plus *Topeka Public Library* and *Topeka Library*. These three terms catch almost everything.

Zappos

Zappos is often mentioned as a great example of a company that knows how to interact with its customers online. Here's how the company does it: "Listening. We've always had a great feedback loop at Zappos.com, through our conversations with you on our 1800 number (1-800-927-7671), Facebook, Twitter, blog comments, surveys and testimonials, we get a pulse of how you are doing and how we are doing. We're going to continue to listen to your feedback and be actively asking for your input on existing and new site features. Every comment is read, often multiple times, by different people and a lot of the feedback we get from you start discussions and define what we work on. Keep the comments coming because it's one way to inform the team if we're on the right track and doing the right things."[2]

Zappos doesn't listen passively. The company actually asks customers for input on website features. Then, it uses that information to start discussions and define what it's going to work on. In Zappos's case, a little conversation plus a lot of listening helps improve business.

David Weinberger

Book authors have found value in online listening, too. Back in 2007, I read David Weinberger's book *Everything Is Miscellaneous*. The book made me think, so I blogged about it—a two-part series of posts (you can find the first here—www.davidleeking.com/2007/07/03/thoughts-on-everything-is-miscellaneous-part-1).

Guess what? David Weinberger commented on *both posts*. We don't know each other. He simply had listening feeds set up for his name and probably for the title of his book. I found that pretty darn cool—cooler still that the author not only listened to what readers were saying, but that he would jump into the conversation taking place.

Hanging in Your Customers' Space

In each of these examples, people/organizations are listening to their customers. In some cases, though, they are going one step further and responding to those customers. That type of listening requires an organization or a person to be in the customer's space, either directly by subscribing or by setting up alerts for the organization's name (or product and service names) and listening to what people—their customers—say about them.

Why Listen?

This brings us to the question: Why listen? Why in the world would you subject yourselves to listening to customer complaints? Those can be bad enough when the customer is complaining in person. But on the web, they're *not* in your face. They might be having a "private" conversation with friends, and you're just (digitally) eavesdropping!

There are two reasons to listen in to these conversations online:

1) *You can't do anything about it if you don't listen.* Suggestions and criticisms are generally a good thing. Organizations can gather and use them to improve their services and products by acting on what they've heard from customers. Good organizations have always done this, but the web just makes it much easier to do. Easy-to-use self-publishing tools enable people to share their

thoughts online, and your customers are doing just that. They share about their interactions with your organization, whether or not their perceptions accurately reflect your organization.

If you're *not* listening, you can't respond. You can't correct bad information, and you can't thank a customer for good information. You certainly won't be able to interact with your online customers. You *must* listen in order to respond.

2) *It connects you to your customers.* A small business receives comments about products and services all the time from people who walk into their stores or start using their services. At the library, people comment all the time about the library as they're checking out books or asking a question.

Online, it's much harder to overhear customers talking about you, even if they're at your digital store (i.e., visiting your website). Generally, this won't happen unless you actively seek it out. Setting up listening feeds gives you the opportunity to hear what your customers like about you and your stuff—how they really feel about it. If you're listening for these types of interactions, you can correct bad information and thank people for liking your products. Use the information you learn to improve your business.

Listening Tools

Here are some individual tools useful for online organizational listening. I'll look in-depth at a couple and then list other useful listening tools toward the end of this chapter.

Twitter

Twitter is a great listening tool, and there are a few different ways to listen using Twitter. One easy way to see what people are saying about you is to monitor Twitter for comments about company or products, which can happen in two ways: mentions and retweets

(RTs). Every time someone mentions you in Twitter and uses your Twitter name (e.g., *@topekalibrary*), the owner of that Twitter name sees that message in his Twitter reader.

RTs happen when someone reposts someone else's complete Twitter message. For example, let's pretend I just posted this to my Twitter account: "I love working at @topekalibrary!" If someone else who loves the library RTs that post, it might look something like this: "@anotherperson I love the library too! RT @davidleeking I love working at @topekalibrary!" The library would be notified of both posts, because its name was mentioned in each one.

This allows you to see what people are finding interesting enough about your organization to actually pass it on to their Twitter followers. It's a good way to gauge interest in your organization's offerings and in your staff's customer service skills. If you get a lot of mentions or RTs on a new product, service, or even a blog post, then you have probably hit a nerve. You should think about doing more with that idea or service because Twitter mentions show interest by your customers.

By far the greatest listening tool in Twitter is Twitter Search. Go to search.twitter.com and experiment. This simple but powerful search box finds keywords in Twitter status updates.

There are a few ways you can set up searches. For example, I have set up searches for *topeka library*. That phrase catches most iterations of our organization's name, including *Topeka & Shawnee County Public Library, Topeka Library,* and *Topeka and Shawnee County Public Library*.

I just checked my saved search for *topeka library*. Here's what I see: a group of aspiring filmmakers meeting in our cafe, a couple of media outlets pointing to a blood drive we're sponsoring next week, someone mentioning our mobile app for a Symbian smartphone, someone mentioning one of my presentations about the library, and someone talking about picking up a horror novel at the library.

This tells me that people are interested in the library's programs, that they're successfully using our meeting facilities, and that customers like our genre fiction collection. Good stuff to know.

You can go further with Twitter Search. In this initial search, I was just looking for my organization's name. With Twitter Search, you can also create searches on topics of interest to your organization, so I'll stick with the library example here. If I go to Twitter's Advanced Search (Figure 5.1), I can search by ZIP code and then narrow those results with keywords.

For the library, I might create a search for the word *reading* and add Topeka's ZIP code, which is 66604. This search finds people reading the Bible, mystery novels, and campaign notes. This type of search can be used as a very simplistic market segmentation research tool to show what local Twitter users (which can roughly equal people with easy access to technology tools) like to read. From there, TSCPL can provide more of those types of books.

Facebook

Facebook is similar to Twitter when you start with the status update box. The main difference between the Twitter and Facebook status update boxes is that comments on a Facebook status update are easier to follow. Facebook status update comments are included below the actual post.

Because of this, Facebook status updates are fun to use. Treat Facebook similarly to Twitter and ask a question. Assuming that your Facebook friends are active Facebook users, you will most likely receive responses to your question. So, ask wisely!

Facebook also allows people to "Like" status updates and the comments left on those status updates. A Like can show that people are interested in the comments or that they appreciate an idea or a new service. At the very least, Likes serve as a rough gauge of interest in the idea.

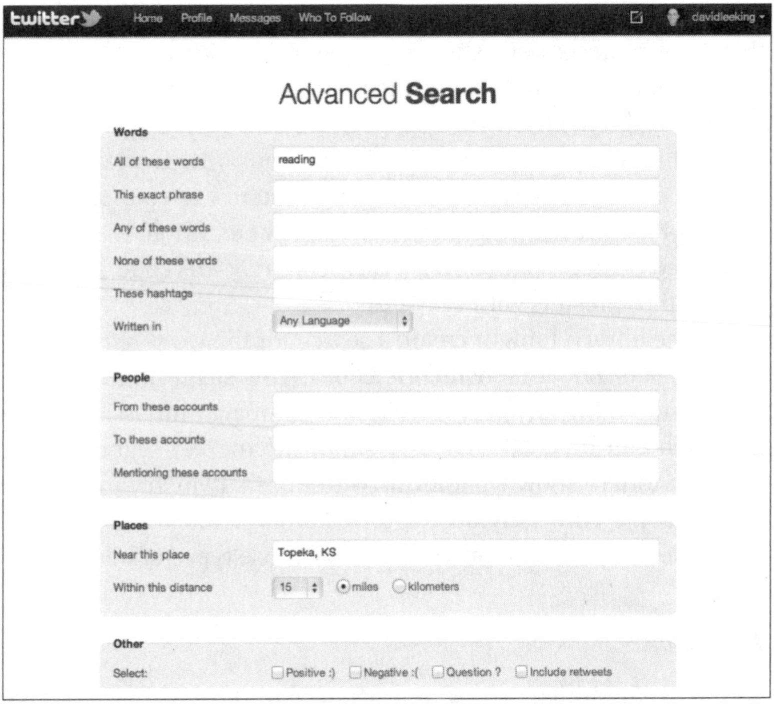

Figure 5.1   Advanced Twitter Search options

Facebook Pages include analytics, called Insights, which meas-ure activity on your Facebook Page (Figure 5.2). Insights measure New Likes, Lifetime Likes, the number of monthly active users of your Page, interactions such as Post Views and Post Feedback, gender and age of your users and where they live, and external referrers.

Insights are a great way to craft your content to meet your cus-tomers' needs. For example, the Gender and Age Insights might show that your average Facebook Page viewer is a 35-year-old female. With that information, you can target your Facebook Page content to that type of persona (your average 35-year-old female

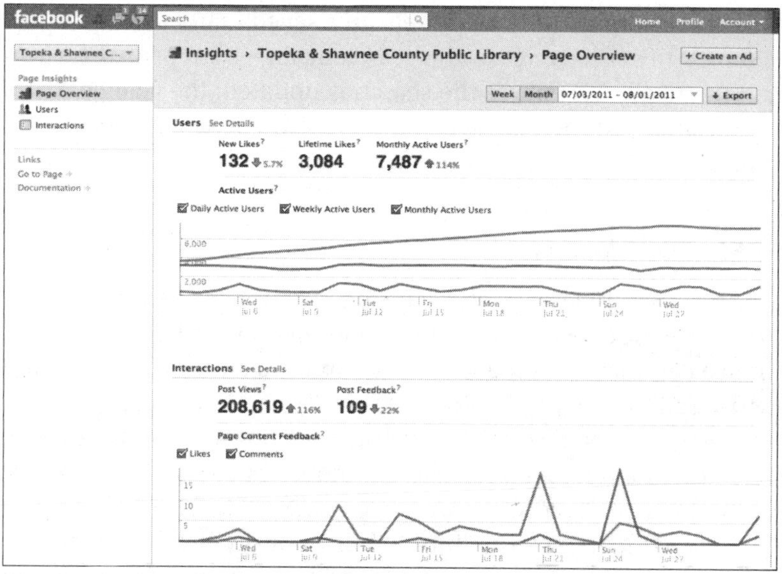

Figure 5.2   Facebook Insights results page

customer). What would that person be interested in, relative to your organization? You might find that by tailoring your Facebook content to your predominant user type, you generate more interaction from that user group.

Google Alerts

Another great listening tool is Google Alerts. Go to www.google.com/alerts and do a search for your business name. There are a number of options to choose from, including setting an alert for everything or narrowing down to blog posts or news stories, deciding how often alerts should be delivered, and specifying if all search results or just the best search results are delivered to you. Select your favorite delivery method (email or an RSS feed), and you are all set!

Subscribing to these alerts sets up a saved search on that topic. You don't ever have to do the search again—it's repeated for you automatically. Whenever the search is updated, the Google Alerts feed sends you the latest search results. Using Google Alerts is a simple way to listen to customers.

Other Ways to Listen

The tools we just learned about are forms of what I'll call *direct listening*. Someone typed out a comment and left it somewhere—in Twitter or in a comment to someone's blog—and you received a copy of the conversation. You can also do what I call *indirect listening*. Indirect listening uses the same tools, but instead of setting up searches for your organization, you set up searches for industry buzzwords. Think of it as business intelligence research, and you'll get the idea.

Visual listening can be fun, too. It basically involves watching for mentions of your business, products, or services in online photo and video sharing sites like Flickr or YouTube. On these sites, you can watch for people unpacking their new toys that they bought from you—then congratulate them on their purchase. You might watch for a video of someone using your services for the first time or listen for people complaining about your organization via a video or a photo. Set up similar listening alerts, then watch and respond as needed. Flickr lets you subscribe via RSS to tag searches. YouTube has similar capabilities: Do a search in YouTube, and then copy and paste the URL of your search into an RSS Reader (like Google Reader). You are now subscribed to that YouTube search.

What to Listen For?

So far, we have discussed what online listening is and how to listen in a variety of ways. What exactly should you be listening for?

Mentions

The most obvious thing to listen for is mentions of your organization's name or a brand, product, or service related to your organization. Listen for people using your products and services.

Listen for industry buzzwords—and for the competition! Are you a bakery? Listen to what people say about *other* bakeries and then improve on the things that people don't like about those bakeries.

Who Is Speaking

When listening, also figure out who is "speaking." Is it a local or industry influencer? Maybe you should listen a little more closely. Is it a power user who loves what your organization does? Work with that customer to make her happy, because she will share what you did with her online friends and followers.

How about people asking, "Hey, has anyone tried this thing out from so and so company?" These are potential customers. If you hear that question, respond.

Where They're Talking

Listen for where the conversation is taking place. Is it on a blog? On Twitter? In a specific forum? Maybe you should watch those online places a little more closely. What part of the country or service area are commenters from? You can usually discover this by taking a quick look at a person's profile.

Find out where the conversation is taking place and then go where those people are gathering. Start talking there.

When Is the Time to Respond?

The next question you should be asking is this: "When should I respond, or should I respond at all?" Usually, a response is great. A customer has asked a question, and what's not to like about the organization actually answering that question? A response isn't always necessary, however. Sometimes, it's good enough to listen and get a feel for activity surrounding your organization.

Explanations, clarifications, and corrections are generally useful responses. While it's certainly OK to gently correct inaccurate information about your organization, remember to be kind and professional in the response.

Disagreeing with someone is OK, too. Not everyone will like your products, and they will say so. That's OK. Remember to relax, and don't take the criticism personally. Above all, remember that you are representing your organization. Put on your best face, and respond with the weight and the persona of the organization behind you, rather than based on how the comment makes you feel.

Thanking customers for using a service, or for buying a product and mentioning it, can also be useful. This type of response shows the customer that the organization listens and cares. Responding helps build those face2face connections and will keep the customer coming back for more.

Listening Tools

Now let's look at some listening tools. We've already talked about some basic listening tools, including Twitter, Facebook, and Google Alerts. There are some other handy tools out there that also help in the listening process.

Message Boards

Discussions are happening right now on thousands of online message boards and discussion groups, and these aren't always picked up in normal search engines. Thankfully, there are a couple of tools that do pick up those conversations. Check out BoardTracker, BoardReader, Omgili, Google Groups, and Yahoo! Groups. Each of these has a search engine feature that searches across forums and newsgroups.

Message Boards

BoardTracker, www.boardtracker.com
BoardReader, www.boardreader.com
Omgili, www.omgili.com
Google Groups, www.groups.google.com
Yahoo! Groups, www.groups.yahoo.com

Aggregator Tools

There are a number of tools that aggregate social media and blog content mentions, provide statistics, and give insights. Some are free, and some have a cost.

Free Aggregators

BackType allows you to set up alerts for social media mentions, then follow those alerts via either an RSS feed or an email alert. BackType finds some conversations that don't seem to get picked up in many other places, like discussions happening in FriendFeed. BackType has been acquired by Twitter, so time (and Twitter) will tell how long this service will exist.

Another free aggregator is Postling, which claims it's "the easiest way to connect with your customers" (from its website). The site has a basic account that's free, as well as fee-based accounts for premium services. Postling does a lot of things, including publishing to multiple platforms in one handy place. You can post to your blog, Facebook, Twitter, Tumblr, LinkedIn, and Flickr. Comments left on your blog, Facebook, Twitter, or Flickr can all be read and responded to within Postling, which, if you receive a lot of comments, might save you some time. Postling has a dashboard view of recent posts and comments received, so you can view them in one place (and reply to them by simply clicking the Reply button).

Postling notes this about listening: "You've told us how important it is to know every time your business is mentioned on the web. With Postling Tracking, we dig through Twitter, blogs, mainstream media, RSS feeds and more to find every time your name comes up. With a single click, you'll be able to share that tweet or writeup in the local newspaper to your blog, Facebook, or Twitter. Are there certain phrases that you know lead to potential new customers? Want to spy on your competition? Save those phrases within Postling Tracking and we'll notify you when you've got a match."[3]

Addictomatic is a free aggregator as well. Here's how it describes itself: "Addictomatic searches the best live sites on the web for the latest news, blog posts, videos and images. It's the perfect tool to keep up with the hottest topics, perform ego searches and feed your addiction for what's up, what's now or what other people are feeding on."[4]

Basically, Addictomatic is a customized start page. When you do a search with Addictomatic's search engine, you are presented with individual search boxes. Each box represents a search in social tools and search engines like Twitter, Bing, Google, or YouTube. You can move the boxes around on the page, and add or delete boxes from different sources. This offers a great, visual way to stay up-to-date on what people are saying about you. Run the search, bookmark the page, and check it out regularly.

The free aggregator Social Mention is a "social media search and analysis platform that aggregates user generated content from across the universe into a single stream of information. It allows you to easily track and measure what people are saying about you, your company, a new product, or any topic across the web's social media landscape in real-time. Social Mention monitors 100+ social media properties directly including: Twitter, Facebook, FriendFeed, YouTube, Digg, Google, etc."[5]

Perform a search in Social Mention, and here's what happens:

- The middle column represents mentions. These mentions come from all over, unless you have narrowed the results down to individual sites, like Twitter or blogs. Each search result includes a little graphic showing where the search is coming from (Twitter, Ask, Google, etc.).

- The left column includes a set of social media analytics, like sentiment (it measures positive versus negative comments), top keywords, top users, top hashtags, and sources.

- The right-hand column includes alert feeds, so you can subscribe to the search via an RSS feed or an email alert. You can also download a CSV/Excel file of the search and the sentiment, top keywords, top users, and top hashtags data.

Free Aggregator Tools

BackType, www.backtype.com
Postling, www.postling.com
Addictomatic, www.addictomatic.com
Social Mention, www.socialmention.com

Desktop Aggregators

TweetDeck, HootSuite, and Seesmic are three tools that started out as desktop-based Twitter tools but have turned into multisite social conversation aggregators. Each tool has a multicolumn view, so you can arrange your Twitter followers in different ways, including all followers, mentions, direct messages, specific searches, and lists.

Each of these are handy listening tools, because you can set them up to follow multiple social media accounts. This lets you have one place to go to follow conversations in multiple Twitter accounts, Facebook, LinkedIn, and Foursquare, for example.

Desktop Aggregators

TweetDeck, www.tweetdeck.com
HootSuite, www.hootsuite.com
Seesmic, www.seesmic.com

Fee-Based Aggregators

Want more stats, more customization? Then you might want to consider a fee-based listening tool. Some popular ones include Spiral16, Radian6, and Viralheat. These services provide listening and responding tools that multiple users can access, like an organizational site license. They also provide statistics and insights on social media, and some provide customized reports.

I suggest starting with the free tools. Then, if you want more control over comment responses or want analytic reports that can be emailed to management, you might want to consider moving to one of these fee-based monitoring and insight measurement tools.

Fee-Based Aggregators

Spiral16, www.spiral16.com
Radian6, www.radian6.com
Viralheat, www.viralheat.com

Change Is (Always) in the Air

Remember: By the time you read this, at least one of these tools will have probably changed or closed shop (though I'll try my darndest to update it as close to printing as possible). In the modern web, changes happen fast, and that's OK. Don't limit yourself. Try multiple listening and measuring tools. Find ones that give you what your business needs and adapt as needed.

Endnotes

1. Chris Brogan, "Listen: The Importance of Bigger Ears," Success Magazine Blog, August 19, 2010, accessed January 24, 2012, blog.success.com/experts/chris brogan/listen-the-importance-of-bigger-ears.

2. Alex Kirmse, "A Conversation With the Customer—Listen, Watch, Learn and Tell," Zappos Blogs: Technology, January 31, 2011, accessed January 24, 2012, blogs.zappos.com/blogs/technology/2011/01/31/conversation-customer-listen-watch-learn-and-tell.

3. Postling, "Postling Tour: Reach People," accessed January 24, 2012, www.postling. com/tour_reach.php.

4. Addictomatic, "About Addictomatic," accessed January 24, 2012, www.addicto matic.com/about.

5. Social Mention, "About Social Mention," accessed January 24, 2012, www.socialmention.com/about.

CHAPTER

6

Business Casual

I have to admit that I enjoy wearing casual clothes more than formal clothes. Dressing casually relaxes me and helps me feel a little
bit more like, well, *me*. I'll take blue jeans over dress slacks any day.

Organizations can also come across as either formal or casual in
their communications to customers. Formality is a quick way to
kill any hint of a personal touch in corporate communications to
customers. Your customers want to connect with your organization, and being a little more organizationally casual in interactions
on the web can help. This chapter explains how to let your organization's personality hang out a bit in order to help your customers
feel comfortable connecting with you.

Examples of Informality in Action

Let's look at some examples of organizations that use an informal
tone to sell their products.

Pike Place Fish Market

Ever been to Pike Place Market in Seattle, Washington? If so, you've most likely seen the Pike Place Fish Market. It's the corner fish market, and you really can't miss it. They have a well-known habit of throwing customers' orders across the shopping area (Figure 6.1).[1] A typical routine involves a customer ordering a fish and the employees calling out the order, which is loudly shouted back by all the other staff. Then an employee throws the customer's fish behind the counter to be wrapped. While working, the staff continually yells to each other and chants in unison while they throw ordered fish. Sometimes, they get a customer from the crowd to participate in the fish toss as well. It's quite fun to watch and tends to attract onlookers.

The fun continues on the company's website (www.pikeplace fish.com). It features a webcam, so you can watch the action. It uses fun, informal text, like "Can't be here with us? We'll bring the market to you!" or "Valentine's Day is almost here. Don't forget to place your orders today. Nothing says 'I Love You' better than a box full of fish."[2] Pictures of employees and customers pepper the site, while the employee page shows pics of each staff member with full names and little tidbits of fun information.

Here's what the company says about itself:

> We asked ourselves, "What does this mean—being world famous?" And we created our own definition. For us it means going beyond just providing outstanding service to people. It means really being present with people and relating to them as human beings. You know, stepping outside the usual "we're in business and you're a customer" way of relating to people and intentionally being with them right now, in the present moment, person to person. We take all our attention off ourselves to be only with them … looking for ways to

Figure 6.1   Tossing the "merchandise" around is Pike Place Fish Market's unusual strategy for attracting customers

serve them. We're out to discover how we can make their day. We've made a commitment to have our customers leave with the experience of having been served. They experience being known and appreciated whether they buy fish or not. And it's not good enough just to want that—it takes an unrelenting commitment. We've made it our job to have that experience happen for every customer. To us, being "World Famous" is a way of being. You can't manualize it. It gets created by each one of us, newly every time. It comes out differently for different people. It also depends on who the customer is … how they react. It's about taking care of people. We're always on the lookout for how we can make a difference in people's lives.[3]

Southwest Airlines

At an airport, I once saw people (mostly kids) lined up at the window staring at one of Southwest's three planes painted to resemble Shamu, the orca at Sea World. Kids were excited to ride on that plane! The fun at Southwest Airlines doesn't stop with orca-painted airplanes, and you can find videos of singing flight attendants on YouTube. One is titled "Funny Steward Southwest Airlines Rapping Safety Information." Yes, you read that right: a video of a rapping airline attendant. If you've ever flown Southwest, while you might not have experienced the rapping flight attendant, you probably have experienced some lightheartedness. The attendants frequently tell jokes or do something else out of the ordinary.

Southwest's mission statement explains why: "The mission of Southwest Airlines is dedication to the highest quality of Customer Service delivered with a sense of warmth, friendliness, individual pride, and Company Spirit."[4] Southwest wants its customers to feel comfortable, and Southwest employees work hard to put their customers at ease.

Customer service at Southwest combines an informal, fun atmosphere and value-added services—like no bag fees and $5 in-flight Wi-Fi service. Not surprisingly, Southwest regularly wins awards for customer service.

Einstein Bros Bagels

A couple of years ago, I was eating at an Einstein Bros Bagels and noticed that the container of honey almond cream cheese was called "Honey Almond Shmear" (Figure 6.2). That prompted me to notice the other words and phrases Einstein Bros uses on its marketing copy: It loves to be informal! In fact, all of its cream cheese flavors are called "shmear."

Take a peek at the company's Quick Casual page (under "Our Company"), which explains its "quick casual" concept: "From cozy, warmly lighted lunch cafes with comfy chairs and community tables to convenient counter-order bagel delis, ENRG [Einstein Noah Restaurant Group] offers an array of quick casual options."[5] The page mentions words like casual, neighborhood, comfortable, friendly, and community. I love how the company takes the concept

Figure 6.2 Informally named "Honey Almond Shmear" cream cheese

of "quick casual" dining—better than fast food, but still fast—and makes its language match that casual atmosphere, while still clearly expressing what it is you're getting.

Pike Place Fish Market, Southwest Airlines, and Einstein Bros all share some similarities. Each is adapting a casual, light, yet still professional attitude in its business-to-customer dealings. Communication is fun and casual, but it is still knowledgeable and professional. These businesses are able to successfully strike a balance between being too casual and too formal, and they end up connecting with their customers in the process. They use casual, comfortable language, and they use people skills to help put their customers at ease or even to entertain them. The experience they create feels comfortable and pleasant—and it keeps people coming back for more.

Translating Informality to the Web

I'm not the only one who thinks that adapting a casual and fun attitude equals approachability—and more sales. For example, the Missouri Small Business & Technology Development Center lists informality as one characteristic of an effective team. It notes that in an effective team, "the climate tends to be informal, comfortable and relaxed. There are no obvious tensions or signs of boredom."[6] While this is talking about an internal business team, the same theory also applies when communicating business-to-customer.

Clare Lancaster, writer at Darren Rowse's blog (www.problogger. net), thinks that using a human voice and personal phrasing, rather than adapting a formal, professional voice, is imperative in connecting with people via the web. She says, "The increase in spam bots that are infiltrating social networks means that people are becoming more cautious. You need to use a human voice (more casual than corporate) if you want people to connect with you."[7] Georgina Laidlaw, another writer at ProBlogger, agrees. She says: "If you want to be your readers' friend, sound like one. That means: stay away from jargon, explain things in user-friendly language, and avoid language designed to imply that you're experienced or skilled—if you are those things, just say so up front."[8]

Surprisingly, even a traditional corporate giant like Microsoft shares these sentiments. Here's how the company describes the language used on its Microsoft Surface project: "Casual language is familiar, informal, conversational, natural, colloquial, and sometimes idiomatic. Use casual and comfortable language in Microsoft Surface applications, but avoid overly colloquial or idiomatic language that fails to add clarity and increases localization costs."[9]

Ways to Keep It "Real"

The following are some techniques you can use to stay informal while remaining professional.

Write Like You Talk

Most of us learned that writing needs to be formal and proper; we were taught to write business letters and academic papers. Now, I'm basically asking you to forget most of those lessons. This is very hard for some people to do. We've been trained to write a certain way, so writing in a different way doesn't come naturally. We do better when we keep this rule of thumb in mind: Write like you talk.

Logan Zanelli at Copyblogger agrees:

> Use the same words that you do in your everyday life. If you write the way you talk, you'll be more inclined to use common, everyday words that you would normally use in conversation. This prevents you from sounding like Captain Jack Sparrow using (in my best Johnny

Depp impersonation) obtuse and generally confounding speech that makes your readers wish they were drinking rum. So keep your writing simple and clear without artificially inflated language. A good rule of thumb is: If the average person would need a dictionary to know what your word means, then you need a different word.[10]

Say It Out Loud

If writing like you talk is hard for you, here's a simple trick to help get you there: Simply say it out loud. Read, out loud, what you just typed. Does it sound like you? Or does it sound like Zanelli's Captain Jack Sparrow?

If it does, rewrite your text so it sounds like *you*, talking.

Write to a Friend

Pretend you're writing to your best friend or to a sibling. Think about that for a minute—when you're writing an email or a Facebook message to a friend, do you use formal language? I'm guessing not. Instead, you probably write a bit more casually, as if you are standing there, talking to your friend. You're familiar with that person, so you are using casual, friendly language with them.

That's the very same voice you need to use—minus the inside jokes and potentially off-color language—when writing to customers.

Wear Fun Clothes—Not a Suit and Tie

If you're a visual person, here's another way to think about this concept. Picture your writing like a person wearing casual clothes, rather than a tuxedo. This is another trick to help you remove formal language from your writing—write like it's "casual Friday" rather than "meeting Monday." Since it's your organization we're talking about, write "business casual"—a more casual voice but still representing a professional, competent organizational voice to your customers and website visitors.

Use Your Real Voice, Not Your "Professional Voice"

I've known a few people who have two voices when they talk to people: one voice, or persona, for what they deem more professional settings, and another, more casual, let-it-all-hang-out voice or persona when they're hanging out with friends.

In fact, I had a communications professor who loved to use two voices—one more professional and one more colloquial. My professor for voice and articulation had a huge Texas drawl, which she had tamed for the most part. She had also worked on lowering her voice pitch, so that she sounded very neat, proper, and professional. That voice was her formal voice.

Some of her students, however, liked to tease the drawl back out of her. We worked pretty hard to get her laughing. If we succeeded, she'd get worked up a bit, then let out a high-pitched, drawl-infused guffaw that was definitely worth it. That hoot of laughter was the personality behind the professional presentation.

My point here? Use your "real" voice—not your toned-down professional one. People want to see, hear, and read the real you. Sure, you should probably temper it some, so you sound business casual, not weekend casual. But work on letting some of the authentic "you" out. In using your authentic voice, people will connect with you and with your company.

Use Language Your Customers Use

To sound informal, you need to remove the technical language and jargon from your site. (In the library setting I work in, we have to really work at this one—and most businesses are in the same predicament, because of industry jargon.) An easy way to do this is to simply ask your customers what they'd call something. For example, we removed one bit of jargon at my library just by asking our customers what they would call "the room where we put a book they reserved to be checked out." To find out, we stationed one of our marketing interns by our checkout line for a day and had her poll the people waiting in line. We received some great feedback—the room is now called the "Holds Pickup Room" and it works well. Our customers know what to look for, because we named it using our customers' language.

You can do a similar thing with your organization's products and services. Pick something your customers use, and simply ask them what they'd call it. For example, I'm sitting in a Starbucks right now. I'll bet you that if the employees here asked all their customers what they should call the "middle-sized drink," most people would say "medium" and not "grande."

Just sayin'.

Social Media

So, that covers websites and blogs. But what about social media sites like Facebook or Twitter? Does this same concept of "business casual" language hold true on social media sites and tools? I think so, but there are a few differences to be aware of.

When talking with customers on social media sites, especially the ones with a status update box, such as Twitter, Facebook, LinkedIn, or Foursquare, be short, to the point, and slightly informal.

Informality on social media sites, though, is not the same thing as being flippant, rude, or argumentative. Sometimes, being polite is hard to do. Customers can be mean. Sometimes, one person's fun and casual attitude is another person's rude and obnoxious attitude.

Because of this, you still need to stay professional. How can you be professional yet stay casual at the same time? Think about an Apple Store employee. When you visit an Apple Store, the floor staff is nice, professional, and knowledgeable (and probably a little biased toward Apple products). But otherwise, they're pretty darn authentic. They're just being themselves—but they happen to be wearing a Genius T-shirt and working at the Apple Store.

We need to be the same way online. That's why I say to take on a business casual attitude in your organizational writing, especially to customers. A more casual, authentic voice helps convey your great information to your customers. It just does it in a more understandable and friendly way.

Photos and Videos

Pulling off a business casual attitude visually can be tricky. But there are also ways to be casual and authentic, yet professional, in both photos and videos.

Think about creating some behind-the-scenes videos, showing what goes on in the office or behind-the-scenes. This type of video captures workers in their element (at the office, doing their work), rather than artificially standing in front of a backdrop, with lights shining on them, talking to a camera. You can even interview employees and have them talk to you. Blip.tv employees did a great job of this with their Blip on Blip video series (www.blip.tv/blip-on-blip). They walked around their workplace, taking videos of their staff and sharing those videos with the Blip.tv community.

This type of video shows real people at work, having fun. Getting to know someone by watching him in a video helps customers. When customers have to call in for support, for example, they might just "know" who they're talking to—because they just saw that customer service rep online.

Your Organization, Not Yourself

Finally, remember this: When you share that slightly casual, personal voice while interacting online on behalf of your organization, you are essentially representing that organization. You become the voice for your organization or business.

Your website, your content, and your employees have unique personalities. This uniqueness will come out. Your brochures were written by people who have a voice, and some personality comes from those, too. All that adds up to an organizational personality. Even your physical building (if you have one) has a feel or personality.

The challenge is to make these personalities match so you can present a uniform image. Sit down, do some planning, and map out each aspect of your organization—the building, the marketing, the website, the staff. Plan the voice of your organization.

Endnotes

1. Photo by Alaskan Dude, accessed January 25, 2012, www.flickr.com/photos/72213316@N00/4108139464.

2. Pike Place Fish Market homepage, accessed January 25, 2012, www.pikeplacefish.com.

3. "How We Became World Famous," Pike Place Fish Market, accessed January 25, 2012, www.pikeplacefish.com/about/world-famous.

4. "About Southwest," Southwest Airlines, accessed January 25, 2012, www.southwest.com/html/about-southwest/index.html.

5. "About ENRG: Quick Casual," Einstein Noah Restaurant Group, Inc., accessed April 10, 2012, www.einsteinnoah.com/about/quickcasual.aspx.

6. Rick Sparks, "Characteristics of an Effective Team," Missouri Small Business & Technology Development Centers, April 2002, accessed January 25, 2012, www.missouribusiness.net/sbtdc/docs/characteristics_effective_team.asp.

7. Clare Lancaster, "The 5 Critical Errors Most People Make When They Start Using Social Media for Business," ProBlogger, December 16, 2010, accessed January 25,

2012, www.problogger.net/archives/2010/12/16/the-5-critical-errors-most-people-make-when-they-start-using-social-media-for-business-2.

8. Georgina Laidlaw, "Save the Sanctimony: Make Your Blog Sound Like a Trusted Friend," ProBlogger, September 10, 2010, accessed January 25, 2012, www.problogger.net/archives/2010/09/10/save-the-sanctimony-make-your-blog-sound-like-a-trusted-friend.

9. "4.2.1 Using a Casual Comfortable Tone," Microsoft, accessed January 25, 2012, www.msdn.microsoft.com/en-us/library/ff318667%28v=surface.10%29.aspx.

10. Logan Zanelli, "7 Tips for an Authentic and Productive Writing Process," Copyblogger, accessed January 25, 2012, www.copyblogger.com/authentic-writer.

Design and Face2Face Connections

Friendly, customer-focused design is inviting and helps customers feel welcome in a physical space. This principle holds true online as well. In this chapter, let's explore how a well-designed digital experience can help your organization provide that face2face human touch for customers.

Here's an example of friendly design in a physical space. Volkswagen decided to hold a design contest, described at www.thefuntheory.com.[1] In response, a design group in Stockholm, Sweden, chose to address the fact that when an escalator and stairs are side by side, most people take the escalator—despite the health benefits of walking up the stairs instead. So they designed a piano staircase, which was basically an overlay that played musical notes as you stepped on the stairs, much like stepping on the keys of a giant piano. The design group even designed the stairs to look like piano keys.

Guess what this team discovered? Sixty-six percent more people chose the piano stairs over the escalator. It made people smile! Volkswagen created a video showing people's reactions to the musical staircase (www.youtube.com/watch?v=2lXh2n0aPyw). More than one person in the video was shown taking photos or videos of the stairs themselves, and the escalator didn't see a lot of use. Why? Because the design group made using the stairs fun! The group also demonstrated that design, when connected with a sense of fun, can change people's behavior.

Another company that's good at human-focused design is Apple. Take its iPad, for instance. Everyday users like to shoot videos of their toddlers using an iPad,[2] and young children are able to intuitively figure out how to use the touch screens on iPads and iPhones. At the other end of the age spectrum, I have also seen videos of elderly people easily using iPads to look at pictures. The swiping movement that moves pictures around is a familiar action,[3] just like turning the page of a book.

Apple's iOS products—iPads, iPhones, and iPod Touches—are designed to be easy and intuitive to use. Apple focused on creating a human-centered design for these mobile devices and figured out how to make a product that people could use naturally, without a steep learning curve.

Goals for Human-Centered Design

Much design talk these days centers around what's being called "design thinking" and "human-centered design." Let's briefly look at those concepts before we move on.

Design Thinking

"Design Thinking is a methodology for practical, creative resolution of problems or issues that looks for an improved future result." It is the essential ability to combine empathy, creativity, and rationality to meet user needs and drive business success. "Unlike analytical thinking, design thinking is a creative process based around the 'building up' of ideas. There are no judgments early on in design thinking. This eliminates the fear of failure and encourages maximum input and participation in the ideation and prototype phases. Outside the box thinking is encouraged in these earlier processes since this can often lead to creative solutions."[4]

Design thinking doesn't focus specifically on digital activities. Instead, it's more of an overall concept of how to wrap the creative process around a problem that needs design as part of the solution.

Human-Centered Design

"In broad terms, 'user-centered design' (UCD) or 'pervasive usability' is a design philosophy and a process in which the needs, wants, and limitations of end users of a product are given extensive attention at each stage of the design process. User-centered design can be characterized as a multistage problem solving process that not only requires designers to analyze and foresee how users are likely to use a product, but also to test the validity of their assumptions with regard to user behavior in real world tests with actual users. Such testing is necessary as it is often very difficult for the designers of a product to understand intuitively what a first-time user of their design experiences, and what each user's learning curve may look like."[5]

Human-centered design isn't really that different from design thinking. It's just a different perspective to the same problem of making a design that's useful, usable, and human-focused, and it puts the customer at the center of the design rather than the technology.

Some other terms to watch for in this area (there are many more than I'm going to list here) are scenario-based design and human-computer interactions.

Ways to Make Your Design More Human-Centered

So how do we incorporate human-centered design? Try these ideas for starters:

- Design for personas.
- Don't get in your customer's way.
- Make your design match.
- Test usability.
- Give people the next step.
- Be mobile friendly.
- Be deliberate in your design.

The following sections talk about each of these ideas.

Design for Personas

You know what a persona is, right? Here's a Wikipedia definition: "Personas are fictional characters created to represent the different user types within a targeted demographic, attitude and/or behavior set that might use a site, brand or product in a similar way. Personas are a tool or method of market segmentation. The term persona is used widely in online and technology applications as well as in advertising, where other terms such as pen portraits may also be used."[6]

Basically, a persona is a brief story written to describe a fabricated customer. Personas are usually focused on a specific subset of customers, based on demographics of current customer groups (e.g., 40-year-old females) or on potential customer groups that the organization wants to reach.

You Can't Design for Everyone

The first lesson in using personas is that you can't design for everyone. Just like the saying, "If you try to please everyone, you'll end up pleasing no one," if you attempt a design that is too general, you will in essence be designing for no one. It is important to thoughtfully choose a market segment to focus your design on, or you'll probably end up with a design that speaks to the web designer but not necessarily your customers.

Know Your Primary Customer Group

Spend some time researching those who use your product or service. For example, Topeka & Shawnee County Public Library recently participated in a GIS study of our customers and our customer area (a single county in Kansas). It provided us with some great map-based data, including where the greatest number of our customers live. The study also grouped our customers into "market segmentation groups." It even showed us where our noncustomers live in our service area. With this data in hand, we can create personas based on the market segmentation data. We can target our potential customers with content and marketing material based on that user group, and we can tailor webpages to appeal to that market segment.

Don't have the money or staff to do a formal study? Simply watch the people visiting your store or organization, or the people using your services, for maybe a month or so … and take notes.

Write down things like approximate age, gender, with kids or without, and what they're buying or looking at, for starters.

Once you have done or paid for those observations—whether formal or informal—you have enough data to start creating personas out of the broad user groups that visit your business or organization. Write a couple of paragraphs about your fabricated customer. Give her a name and create a brief storyline about her and your services. Include the types of things she likes to do, if she owns a house, and so on. Also write down how she likes to connect with your organization and what she does while there (i.e., buy things or use your services).

You might create scenarios describing a typical day of your persona. Think about the different environments and constraints this person might encounter with your services and your website.

Once you have that one-page story about your persona, design your website to make that person happy. Make certain she knows what to do when she visits your website. Use her language. Use colors and visual designs she likes and would expect. Test the design with real people in that user group, and adjust accordingly. Make that persona happy, and you have just made a huge segment of your customers happy in the process, too.

Can you design for multiple personas at the same time? Of course, and many of us will want to. For example, my library's website works to attract adults, teens, and kids—three very different types of people. This requires different personas to focus various parts of the website on. That said, though, don't go overboard. Remember what I said at the beginning of this section: You can't design for everyone. Choose a handful of primary user groups, and create personas around those groups. People who don't fit those categories will still be attracted to your business (because presumably they still like your stuff); you are just focusing your design energies on a specific target market.

Don't Get in Your Customer's Way

When designing for customers, don't get in their way. If you do, those customers will simply go somewhere else. They will find another tool that is easier to use or makes more sense to them. Your goal is to be their go-to, easy-to-use tool. Here are some ideas to help you succeed.

Design the Important Things First

This concept is kind of like a newspaper's inverted pyramid style for articles: Put the most important things first! Is one of your most important things a blog? Then by all means, focus on the content first. Design the text and the readability of a single blog post first. Make sure the rest of the design blends in, not sticks out.

The graphics and design elements should highlight and support the most important content: the blog text.

Is your most important content descriptions of products you sell? If so, design the item's description page first, including the process for purchasing the item. Then build the rest of the website around that functionality.

Turn On the Light Switch

I'm fond of saying this: Make sure your website is as easy to use as a light switch. Think about that for a second. The goal of a light switch is *not* to showcase the wonders of electricity. It's just designed for instant success—at the flick of a switch. The light enables you to perform the task you want to do in the room, but neither the light nor the switch is an end in itself.

On the web, your "room" is your organization or store or business, and your "light switch" is your website. Don't get so enamored with your design that you lose sight of the fact that the website is simply a vehicle to allow business to happen. Make your website so easy to use that no customer has to puzzle out how to use it. If it's too hard to use, they might just decide to go to another room/store/business.

Be Format Agnostic

Your website needs to function correctly on all modern browsers. You don't have to go back and make things work with older browsers, but if your site doesn't work on a potential customer's computer using his browser of choice, he will find another website that works.

Curious to see what browsers your customers use? Check your web analytics. The information is there. You can use a free-yet-powerful web analytics tool like Google Analytics (www.google.com/analytics), which my library favors (Figure 7.1), or your web hosting company might have a web analytics tool it uses and can set you up with an account.

Make Your Design Match

As mentioned earlier, all elements of your business should have a united look. This includes your physical space, your print pieces, your staff uniforms, and the website. You want brand recognition, which, of course, is the idea behind company logos. It would be a rare American who wouldn't recognize McDonald's yellow arches, and those arches are on all of its products, stores, uniforms, and websites.

So, when you're designing your organization's website, your brochures, or even your office space, try to create a visual theme throughout. (This, of course, means that you have to sit down and actually plan that theme!) Visual unity gives the impression of professionalism. It lends you credibility, whereas a disjointed look gives more of an amateur, start-up impression. On the web, in print, and in person: It matters.

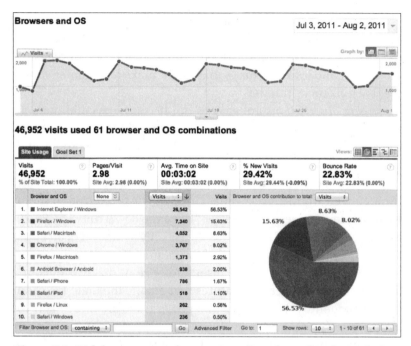

Figure 7.1   Web browsers used at www.tscpl.org from Google Analytics

Test Usability

Usability helps create that "light switch" effect on your site. Is it easy? Does it work? To figure that out, test your website on actual humans. There are many ways to get feedback from your customers when you're designing a website. These include usability testing, cognitive walkthroughs, on-site observations, and heuristic evaluations.

Usability testing is a technique used to evaluate a website by testing it on users. This is usually done through an administered test that observes how website visitors actually use your website.

Cognitive or heuristic walkthroughs are usability inspection methods that identify usability issues in a website. Basically, walk through a section of your site (for example, finding and purchasing a product) and look for things that might make a customer stumble. Then fix those things.

On-site observations are easy to do: If you have computers at your business or organization, simply watch what people do when they visit your site. Note when they get hung up on something, and then fix those problems.

Realize that you are not expecting every person to move easily through your website every time. There will be user error, so shoot for 80 percent success. Apple says: "Heed the 80-20 rule. The 80-20 rule states that roughly 80% of users use only a handful of an app's features, while only about 20% of users might use most or all of the features. Thinking of your user audience in this way encourages you to emphasize the features that enable the main task and helps you identify the features that power users are more likely to appreciate."[7]

Usability studies can also be done quickly. Choose five to 10 things about your website to test. Then find five or six people (these can be spouses or friends) to test. Simply run them through the test, have them talk out loud, write down what they do, where they go, and so on. Then look for trends in their responses and fix accordingly. Then try another group and make those changes.

Give People the Next Step

One of your main website goals should be to keep people on your site. Be sure your customers and website visitors have things to do while visiting your website; you need to give them a reason to stay. One easy way to do this is to tell them what to do next: What should their next actions be?

Here are some examples of next actions:

- At the end of a search, offer links of related material in addition to the search results list.

- At the end of an article, supply a list of related articles.

- On a product record, create an Amazon-like list of other items purchased by people who purchased this particular item.

Give your customers some next actions, and they just might take you up on the offer … and purchase more in the process.

Be Mobile Friendly

Create a mobile-friendly website. Modern websites need to work on all of your customers' devices, whether that's a PC, a Mac, an iPhone or iPad, or an Android smartphone. Figure 7.2 is a screenshot of devices used at my library's website.

Depending on your organization's needs, being mobile friendly might mean developing a mobile version of your website, or it might mean creating a mobile app that works across popular mobile devices. It really depends on your customers and what you offer. Your website analytics probably measure mobile device use already. Figure out what the most-used mobile devices are for your website, and then develop mobile sites or apps for those devices.

This also means that your organization needs to invest in some mobile technology for testing purposes. It's hard to design for the iPhone, for example, if you don't have one. If you can't buy one of each, ask your staff to test mobile access with their favorite devices. If you have some dependable customers who are willing to beta-test a mobile site, ask them to test and report back—and give them a coupon for their trouble.

When designing for mobile, ask this: What would mobile web visitors want to do on a mobile device that's different from the full website? For example, is there something from your organization

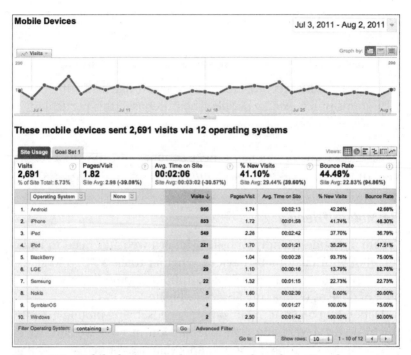

Figure 7.2   Mobile devices used at www.tscpl.org from Google Analytics

that a customer would want to do while standing in line at the grocery store? Those using the TSCPL mobile site can ask quick questions and can renew books online. For your organization, it might mean answering a question about one of your services or browsing a short article about what you're doing.

Your site should work on multiple mobile devices and browsers, so your customers essentially have your organization a pocket's reach away.

Be Deliberate in Your Design

Always bear in mind that your organization needs to design its website for use. There are probably three or four large organizational priorities your website needs to meet. At a library, customers need a way to check out books and ask questions. Coffee shops sell coffee, and possibly mugs and T-shirts. A nonprofit homeless shelter takes donations. Those main priorities need to work flawlessly online. Don't give your customers a reason to walk away.

According to Apple: "The best way to make sure your product meets the needs of your target audience is to expose your designs to the scrutiny of your users. Doing this during every phase of the design process can help reveal which features of your product work well and which need improvement."[8]

Translation? You need to know your audience. Design for those who use your services—your customers.

Endnotes

1. "The Fun Theory," accessed February 24, 2011, www.thefuntheory.com.

2. Telstarlogistics, "A 2.5 Year-Old Has a First Encounter With An iPad," YouTube, April 5, 2010, accessed February 24, 2011, www.youtube.com/watch?v=pT4 EbM7dCMs.

3. Sackr, "Virginia's New iPad," YouTube, April 7, 2010, accessed February 24, 2011, www.youtube.com/watch?v=ndkIP7ec3O8.

4. "Design Thinking," Wikipedia, accessed February 24, 2011, secure.wikimedia. org/wikipedia/en/wiki/Design_thinking.

5. "User-Centered Design," Wikipedia, accessed February 24, 2011, secure.wiki media.org/wikipedia/en/wiki/Human-centered_design.

6. "Persona (marketing)," Wikipedia, accessed February 26, 2011, secure.wiki media.org/wikipedia/en/wiki/Persona_(marketing).

7. User Experience Guidelines," Mac OS X Human Interface Guidelines, accessed April 10, 2012, developer.apple.com/library/mac/#documentation/user experience/conceptual/applehiguidelines/Intro/Intro.html.

8. Ibid.

CHAPTER 8

Face2Face With Specific Tools

The previous chapters introduced face2face connections in relatively general terms. In this chapter, let's delve deeper into blogs, Facebook, Twitter, and YouTube. We'll talk about:

1. What you can do with each tool to connect your organization to your customers

2. How to make human connections while using each service

Blogs

Let's begin with blogs and blogging. Unless you have been hiding under a rock for the last 10 years, you likely know that a blog is basically a website with regularly updated content. It's usually article-driven and has updates in reverse-chronological order so that the newest content appears first. There are usually a variety of ways to subscribe to the blog via its RSS feed or email.

What can you post on a blog? Pretty much anything—text, photos, drawings/pictures, and videos, for starters. There are a variety of ways to make face2face connections with your customers using a blog.

Blog Posts

There are many ways to make customer connections in a blog post. For starters, make your blog posts short. You need to write just enough to get your point across, no more than that. Writing short posts actually leaves room for readers to add their thoughts to your post—and it's good practice to come out and ask readers to share their thoughts.

As in all of your online interactions, use your normal voice when you write. Again, on blogs, try to write like you speak. Some people might have to practice this a bit by actually saying what they want to write out loud first, then writing down what they said.

Include images that support your blog post. For example, if you're writing about a staff person, actually take a picture of Jim the shipping clerk and add that image to the post. If you're describing the process of making chocolate at your candy store, take a photo illustrating the point or perhaps even a video showing the process.

Comments

Comments can be a great way to engage customers. First, enable comments on your blog. Some people, including high-profile bloggers like Seth Godin, choose to keep comments turned off.

That works fine for Seth, but it won't work fine for your business if you are trying to engage your customers.

Then, be daring. Go one step further, and allow customer comments to be posted immediately. Of course, you need to have a spam filter in place, but otherwise, let 'em go. You can always delete a comment after-the-fact, if that comment is offensive. Allowing comments to post automatically will end up saving you time, because you won't have to moderate every comment being posted.

Next, actually respond to the comments left on your blog. Always try to respond on the same day. Why? That comment is the continuation of a conversation. If you don't answer that comment for a few days or more, you have effectively killed the conversation—and killed your customer's engagement.

How do you answer the comments customers leave? It depends on the comment, but generally, your answer will probably look like one or more of these:

- Thanking the customer for the comment

- Answering a question

- Providing added information

Answering comments, even with a simple response like "Hey Joe, thanks for the comment" is useful. It shows you are active and interested, which in turn portrays your organization as one that's active and interested in the needs and thoughts of its customers.

"About Me" Page

Sometimes, you might need an About Me or an About Us page; use an About Me page if you run a small, one-person consulting, freelance, or other type of business. About pages are a great way to introduce yourself, what you do, and how customers can contact you.

I'll use my website at www.davidleeking.com as an example. My two About pages talk about me as a person and about my blog/consulting business. The About This Website information describes what my blog is all about and that I speak and consult about libraries and technology. The separate About Me section describes David Lee King the person.

If you are a larger business, or if you want to focus more on the business end of things and less on employees, you can still create an About Us page. This should, at the very least, include information about what your business does, contact information, and who's in charge. Include some transparency by including first and last names and pictures of staff. Also, follow the same "business casual" writing standards you're following in your blog posts.

Other Pages to Include

If you are a one-person shop (like me), you might include some other interest-based pages besides just an About Me page. For example, I include a page talking about music (and include links to some of my own songs). I include a link to publications I have written for and past presentations I have given. This lets people see what I've done and helps guide them to topics I speak on when they're deciding if I would be a good fit for a conference.

Larger organizations can include a list of relevant information about their business. Some examples of the types of things you might want to include are: an FAQ on a new product, a listing of upcoming events, or even something fun about employees who work at the organization. For example, Zappos includes links to all of its employees' Twitter accounts, so customers can view Zappos employees' interests.

Subscribing

Make sure there are multiple ways to subscribe to your content. Most blogs, for example, should have built-in RSS feeds. Display the link to your RSS feed in an easy-to-access place, so people can find it and easily subscribe. Most blogs place subscriber buttons in the upper right-hand corner of the page.

Not familiar with RSS and RSS feeds? Don't worry—they are really easy to understand. An RSS feed is just a specialized webpage that shows all of your updated content. Many websites and blog software tools create RSS feeds automatically, so it's nothing you need to worry about doing yourself.

RSS feeds are very useful because you can subscribe to them. Find an RSS reader (I use Google Reader at www.reader.google.com). Then subscribe to feeds using your RSS reader (there are many different ways to subscribe, depending on which reader you use). Once you have subscribed to an RSS feed, every time that website updates content, you essentially get a copy of that updated content. Cool, huh?

Allow your readers to subscribe via RSS and via email. Most likely, a large percentage of your customers aren't familiar with RSS or RSS feed readers and won't know what to do with your RSS feed. Thankfully, they *do* understand the concept of subscribing to something, and they most likely have an email account. Provide a way to subscribe to your content through email, and you can pick up more subscribers/customers. For example, my blog has about 500 email subscribers.

Currently, the easiest way to add email subscriptions for your blog is by using FeedBurner, one of Google's many free web tools. FeedBurner's email subscription functionality is easy to set up. Go to feedburner.google.com, then enter your RSS feed URL into the handy "Burn a feed right this instant" text box. Once you have done that, click the Publicize tab, then click Email Subscriptions, and follow the directions there.

Send announcements of blog posts to social media sites like Twitter or Facebook. Some people follow blogs and news sites through social media tools, rather than through RSS or email. When I post an announcement of a new blog post to Twitter, I usually receive comments, retweets, and Likes from Twitter and Facebook readers. I get extra interaction when I post a link to my new content to Facebook.

This is also easy to do. To send blog posts to Twitter and Facebook, use a tool like Twitterfeed (www.twitterfeed.com). Simply set up an account at Twitterfeed, click the Create New Feed button, and then follow the instructions to authorize Twitterfeed to access your Twitter and Facebook accounts. Once done, every time you post a new blog post, Twitterfeed will send a link to that blog post to Twitter and/or Facebook.

Readers click the link on their Facebook Wall, and then leave comments in Facebook, telling me what they think about my newest article. It's yet another way to engage customers.

Facebook

Facebook is currently the second-most popular website in the world, according to Alexa (a website ranking company at www.alexa.com). There are many ways to access Facebook, either through a traditional computer with web access or through a variety of Facebook apps on mobile devices. Many people visit Facebook multiple times a day. In fact, the average person in the U.S. spends approximately 7 hours a month on Facebook.[1]

It's obvious that people spend a lot of time on Facebook. But does Facebook work well for businesses and organizations? Absolutely! Organizations have a great opportunity to interact with customers who enjoy spending time on Facebook.

Basic Information About You

To get an organizational Facebook Page started, go to www.face
book.com/pages and follow the simple three-step process for creating a Facebook Page for your organization. Once your Facebook
Page is created, here are some basic steps to help you get started.

First things first: You need to fill out some basic information
about your organization. This is done on the Information page.
The information you add here will be similar to an About Us page
on a blog. For example, on our Information page, TSCPL includes
information like our hours of operation and our physical location.
We also point back to our main website via a link. Also add a photo
to your Facebook Page that represents your organization. This
could be either your company's logo or (even better) a picture of
your friendly staff. This photo will be used as the Facebook icon
that appears in most of your Page interactions (i.e., status updates,
comments).

Status Update

Facebook is based largely around status updates (also called
Facebook Stories), which allow you to share updates with all your
Facebook friends. Just a quick glance at my Facebook News Feed
(where you'll find your friends' status updates) shows these types
of updates: Someone bought a new shirt while in Istanbul, someone likes Prince (the rock star), and someone else loves his cat
(because he posted pictures). I also noticed that one of my favorite
bloggers just posted a new blog post. Since she has connected her
blog's RSS feed to Facebook, every time she posts something new
on her blog, a link to that blog post is automatically sent to her
Facebook status update—which then gets sent to me, through my
Facebook News Feed.

Organizations can use Facebook to communicate with customers. If you're closed today, let people know. If you're having a

sale, let people know. Ask your customers questions about your business or organization. People will respond.

You can also share cool information about your business, your services, or even your industry. Connect your organization's blog posts into Facebook, so you can share your blog posts with your organization's Facebook friends (who might not be following your blog). After all, those Facebook friends signed up to receive your Facebook content when they Liked your Facebook Page. The process of Liking something in Facebook subscribes that person to your Facebook Page's content, and that Like shows interest in your organization and in your organization's content. So post! You'll have to experiment a bit to find the right amount of status update postings for your Facebook followers. Too many status updates, and people will unfriend you or hide your status updates. Too few, and they'll ignore you. There's no magic number when it comes to how many status updates are acceptable. Find what works best for your organization and your customers by asking them, and then follow that advice.

Comments

Start engaging your Facebook audience, and you will start receiving comments. On Facebook, people can comment on and/or Like each status update. So if you ask a question, chances are good that you will in fact get a reply from a Facebook friend. People might even leave their own questions on your Page's Wall—so you'll need to figure out a plan of attack on how best to answer comments. Who will do the work of answering Facebook comments?

Pictures and Videos

As we talked about in Chapter 6, take pictures or videos of your products, your services, your building, and your staff. Include videos of customers using your product (after getting permission, of course).

Now that you have those pictures and videos, why not share them in Facebook? Let people comment on them. You can even share insider, a-day-in-the-life-of-an-organization content. For example, the Nonprofit Technology Network (NTEN) took pictures of its recent office move and shared the photos on its Facebook Page (find it at www.facebook.com/nten.org).

Sharing Your New Service

Share pics and videos of your new products or services, too. Explain the new service visually with a photo or a video. Then, just like with status updates, respond when someone comments on those photos and videos.

Staff Profiles in Facebook

My guess is that many of your employees have personal Facebook profiles, right? Why not invite them to post about where they work and what they do?

Employees who have a Facebook account most likely use it to share information about the things they're interested in. When they do that, their status update is sent to their personal Facebook network, which is probably not the same as your organization's network. But that employee's personal Facebook network likely includes customers or potential customers for your organization.

So, invite your staff to share the neat stuff they do. Show them how to share your next event in their Facebook status update boxes. Let them answer comments or say they're attending or buying something. (Of course, they should always disclose that they work at your organization.)

Done right, this kind of employee insider sharing can be very powerful. Why? Because the message will be coming from a real friend, rather than from an organization. Those personal recommendations go a long way toward convincing others.

Twitter

Unlike Facebook, Twitter is all about the status update box—because that's all there is to do in Twitter. But, like Facebook, Twitter is also a great way to communicate with people.

You have to interact on Twitter in order to gain followers. Just having an account as a placeholder and occasionally sending out invites to an event won't cut it in Twitter. You have to participate, or no one will follow you.

Profile Picture

Yes, let's start with your profile picture. It's actually pretty important. Why? The profile picture is one of the main visual elements on a Twitter profile page, and the only one that's carried through to other users and in the readers that people use to access Twitter. Since it's the primary visual element that Twitter followers will see, you want to make it count.

If you are a one-person organization or a freelancer, use a quality headshot of yourself for the profile picture. Look straight into the camera lens, so it looks like you are looking at the person viewing your picture/icon. Or, look toward the content, so you're looking to the right when the picture appears on Twitter. It's a little thing, but it makes you look more interested in your readers and your content.

If you are a two- or three-person business, take a picture, as close as you can, of the two or three of you, and use that for your image icon. The goal with these images is to show that there are real people behind the logo or the building. Some larger organizations use their logo, and that can work well, if it's a well-known logo. But if you can use the faces of real employees, that's almost always better. It's one small way to make that human connection easier.

Use a quality photo that reflects your organization well. It's hard to take a business seriously in Twitter if it chooses to represent iteslf with a picture of a dude in a T-shirt eating pizza. (Unless, perhaps, you're a pizza joint.)

Bio

A Twitter profile includes a small space for a short bio, and you want to use that judiciously. In one sentence, share what your business does, what you like, or what you're looking for. Maybe share your mission statement if it's short and memorable. Or simply state why you're using Twitter (i.e., "We're here to share news about us and our services, and to answer questions."). Include a link to your website.

Retweets

Besides just sharing tweets with your followers, you can retweet other people's Twitter postings. Share the interesting content you've discovered. This has the potential to help other potential customers notice your organization, simply because you retweeted something of interest to them. In Twitter, if people are interested in what you share, they will probably friend you.

And, hopefully, that will lead to more business.

YouTube

Video has become a really popular way to share thoughts, new products, and services online. There are certainly other video sites you can use; in addition to YouTube, I have also used Vimeo and

Blip.tv for years. It's generally a good practice to use multiple video platforms because different video sites attract different people and networks, and if one site goes down, you still have some video online.

Let's focus our attention on YouTube for now, though, because it's currently the most popular video service in the world—and it's very simple to use. Your customers already know about YouTube, and many have watched YouTube videos in the past.

Interaction on YouTube

There are a few ways to interact on YouTube. Aside from watching videos, the major way to interact on the site is through comments. Just as on other online services, viewers can leave comments on video content at YouTube. There's a small caveat here, though: Sometimes, the comments people leave on YouTube can be rather juvenile. Because YouTube commenters can be fairly anonymous, this leads to a wide variety of comments, from useful comments to "mean people having a bad day" types of comments.

You can also get real questions, real comments, and some very useful conversations that start through YouTube comments, so respond accordingly. And be nice—even if the other person isn't. Remember, you are representing your organization, not yourself.

YouTube has created an easy way to share YouTube videos with others. Click the Share button, which gives you the option to copy/paste a shortened URL or to send the video to other social media sites like Google+, Twitter, or Facebook. This is an easy way to share your new content with friends and followers in YouTube, and through other social networks.

Friend Invites and Sharing Favorite Videos

Friend invites and clicking a Favorite button are also both great ways to share. Friend invites (besides gathering friends in YouTube that are notified when you post new content) demonstrates your organization's interests. For example, you can friend other non-profits in your city or similar partner organizations. You could also friend some of your YouTube-using customers.

When you mark a video as your favorite, you're not only mark-ing that you liked a video; you can also share these videos with other YouTube users. Videos marked as a favorite can be shared automatically with your friends in other social networks, like Facebook. Then, depending on how you have your Facebook and Twitter relationships set up, that video can automatically be shared from Facebook to Twitter, or vice versa. The ability to quickly share something your organization found interesting with people in three different networks—YouTube, Facebook, and Twitter—is a powerful tool that has the potential to engage your customers who use various platforms.

Channel Page

YouTube accounts all have a main profile page, called the Channel page, which is similar to a profile page in Facebook or Twitter. Here, you should include a similar picture to the one that you use as your avatar/icon in Twitter and in Facebook. It's good practice to use the same picture across social networks to increase brand recognition.

Create a brief paragraph that describes your organization, and create a link back to your website. You can also customize visual elements of the channel page, such as the colors and logo, to match your organization's look and feel.

Location Services

What can you do as an organization with location-based services like Foursquare or the location-based sections of Facebook or

Google+? Quite a bit! These sites are all about introducing people to places. And, in many cases, your organization is a place. For example, you have a store or a service that holds regular meetings. These are perfect places to create a location-based check-in.

First, create a profile for your organization or business in these services. Sign up for the service as an individual first and play with it a bit to understand how the location-based service works. Then start checking out how your customer base or community uses the tool.

Next, set up a profile for your business and start to share some things on your organization's profile page. Share what you do in the tags or in the tips sections. For example, at TSCPL's Foursquare page, we created a tip to "Use one of our databases—get full-text magazine articles!" Foursquare shows that four users have used this service (they get points for using tips).

We also added the following categories and tags to our business profile (some of them were added by our customers).

Categories

- Library
- Cafe
- Bookstore
- Coffee Shop
- High Tech Outlet [*customer addition*]
- College Library [*customer addition*]
- Farmers Market [*customer addition*]

Tags

- Kansas

- Information
- Cafe
- Art Gallery
- Television [*customer addition*]
- Movies
- Coffee
- wifi
- tscpl
- Topeka
- Music
- Questions answered
- DLK [*customer addition*]
- Computers
- Books
- DVDs
- Library

Tags are important for people searching the site while close to your place of business. For example, if visitors to Topeka need to locate a Wi-Fi hotspot and use Foursquare, they can search for *wifi*. They will see that the library is a free Wi-Fi hotspot, because I added the *wifi* tag to our Foursquare profile page.

Fill out the bio and address fields on the profile page. Add a couple of pictures showing your staff and your building. In some of the services, once your organization's address is added to the profile page, a Google map will appear.

The coolest thing you can do with these types of services is to set up a special deal for people who check in or become the "mayor" of a place (that's the person with the most check-ins at a place in Foursquare).

Some businesses create check-in specials. For example, if you visit a restaurant and check in with Foursquare when you get there, you receive a 10-percent-off coupon for the meal. Or, if you become mayor, you might receive a free drink. So be proactive, and set up something special for people who check in and become the mayor. They are people actively using your services and letting you know about it via their check-in. Reward them as the loyal customers they are.

Niche Social Networks

There are many social media tools and sites that are unique to a given industry. For example, a hotel owner might watch sites like Yahoo! Travel and Trip Advisor. Adults looking to reconnect with their high school friends might use Classmates.com or Reunion.com. Book lovers probably know about Goodreads.com, Shelfari, or LibraryThing.

There are hundreds if not thousands of niche social networking sites, focused on very specific industries and hobbies, and some might work well as an addition to your arsenal of social tools. Here are a few lists of niche social networking sites to get you started:

- Niche social networking sites (from convertiv), www. convertiv.com/niche-social-networking-sites

- Top niche social networking sites (from About.com), www.webtrends.about.com/od/socialnetworking/tp/top_ social_networking_sites_s.htm

- 15 niche social networks for niche marketing (from SitePoint), www.sitepoint.com/15-niche-social-networks

Endnote

1. "Facebook Users Average 7 Hrs a Month in January as Digital Universe Expands," Nielsenwire, February 16, 2010, accessed February 14, 2012, blog.nielsen.com/nielsenwire/online_mobile/facebook-users-average-7-hrs-a-month-in-january-as-digital-universe-expands.

CHAPTER
9

Responding to Critics

Many of us have a hard time dealing with criticism, even online criticism doled out by anonymous people. When someone lampoons you or unfairly critiques the project you just poured months or years into, it's generally hard to take.

Some of us get defensive when criticism strikes. Our first inclination is to put out fires and perhaps try to sound "above the fray." Unfortunately, that approach can sometimes sound too much like poorly done, unauthentic PR speak.

On the other extreme, it can be tempting to start calling names, pointing out character flaws, and being just as petty as the commenter. Criticism can feel like fighting words, and when there's a fight, it's natural to put up your dukes and protect yourself—or to strike hard to knock down the opponent before they can do too much damage.

That, of course, is the wrong way to deal with criticism. Please don't be like these examples.

The Snarky PR Agency

Since I blog, I tend to get weird emails once in a while. Lately, I've found my email address on book publisher lists. Someone apparently sold some email lists to a bunch of large and small press publishers. I guess they think that since I'm a librarian, I'm going to be interested in all types of books.

That, of course, is really not the case, as my blog is focused on social media, emerging technology trends, and libraries—sort of a niche market. And although I work in a library, I'm not the person who buys books for the library—that's someone else's job. So, when a publisher sends me these press releases, I find it amusing/irritating/weird—all at the same time.

One day, I had received a bunch of these emails and decided I'd respond to the next one I received. The next one that came in was from a PR agency representing a children's book publisher. So, I fired off an admittedly irritated email reply to them: "Did you even look at my blog? I talk about technology and social media … NEVER anything about children's books. Please remove me from your email list!"

Opportunity #1: I was surprised to receive an email reply: "So sorry for the confusion, I must have the wrong email address for the person I was attempting to reach! Consider yourself removed, No worries." That PR agency followed up with a prompt email, explaining what had happened and correcting the problem. Good for them!

I was wondering if others had received similar emails, so I tweeted this: "Nice. @XXXXXXXXPress [hiding the real name on purpose—they ended up being very professional] just mass spammed me hoping I'd review a kids book. Obviously NEVER read my blog, so why would I read your book?"

Jessamyn West (the cool blogger at www.librarian.net) replied to my tweet with this: "@davidleeking Me too! When I asked nicely to be off the list they said 'there's no list, we just like your blog!' I found it interesting that the PR agency told Jessamyn there was no list and told me there was a list (I assumed that's what "consider yourself removed" meant).

Opportunity #2: That PR agency then replied to my tweets: "@davidleeking wow out for blood on Twitter! nice!" [since deleted]. The opportunity here? The company could have ignored my tweet or could have responded to me and Jessamyn with a short explanation of its "lists." Simple stuff.

Instead, the conversation didn't stop here. The PR agency emailed me, suggesting I was being insensitive on Twitter, and said that "In the future, it wouldn't hurt to take some time to find out where the person sending you an email is coming from. I'm not a mass spammer, just trying to get the book into the right hands. Obviously not yours, you pointed that out."

I emailed back once more, at this point because I was interested in following up. I pointed out the things that had originally been said, such as that I was removed from a list, but that Jessamyn had been told there was no list. I also pointed out that someone, representing the PR agency, had said this to me—"u shouldn't take yurself so seriously" (in a second deleted tweet), and then explained this:

> For the record—I hardly ever take myself seriously—I just find it humorous when PR companies send me mass emails to review books because I'm a librarian, and haven't figured out that IT managers and children's librarians are VERY different. Or they claim they read my blog before sending (which you didn't say, but others have in the past)—obviously not the case, since I

never write about that stuff. And then getting a kinda off-the-cuff, smarty-pants reply that officially came from XXXXXXXXXXX press (since you or someone else sent it using their organizational Twitter account)? And all that because I suggested you spammed me (which you did), and asked a question—"why would I want to read the book?"

This question the PR agency has yet to answer. Bloggers in general like being helpful, but we also like to know someone on the other end actually did their homework first. Just sayin'.

This story will be continued in a moment, because the company actually came through with a great example of positive communication. Before we finish that story though, let's consider what went wrong, and then look at another negative example. First, what went wrong? Well, I obviously did not respond in an exemplary way. I should have let it go and simply deleted the email. I have to admit though, at some point during the conversation, I started thinking that the encounter would be a great example for this book.

The PR agency could have done better by following these suggestions:

1. Don't choose the wrong market: Be sure to do your research before sending a business email. You don't want your communications to be considered spam.

2. Be honest: I questioned this publisher's integrity because my colleague and I were each told different things about the existence of an email list.

3. Don't be drawn into a verbal squabble: I was ranting, and the professional response would either have been to ignore me or just say "Sorry, won't happen again!"

4. Focus on the issue, not the person: If you choose to respond, discuss the problem. Don't make personal suggestions (i.e., "don't take yourself so seriously").

Target and Its Offensive Targets

In 2008, Amy Jussel from ShapingYouth.org wrote a blog post about a Target billboard she found offensive and called the company to complain about it. She included Target's response in her post: "'Unfortunately we are unable to respond to your inquiry because Target does not participate with nontraditional media outlets [blogs] … This practice,' the public relations person added, 'is in place to allow us to focus on publications that reach our core guest,' as Target refers to its shoppers."[1]

Opportunity #1: Did you see what Target did? Target emailed a response that essentially said that the company doesn't respond to nontraditional media outlets. But someone did respond; Target's email to Amy was a response in itself. Target should have either: 1) not responded, or 2) responded with a simple, "Thanks for your inquiry. We'll look into it."

Opportunity #2: Target was already participating with nontraditional media outlets. In 2007, Rosie Siman, 21, was a senior at the University of Georgia and a member of the Target Rounders, which was a group of mostly college students who received discounts, CDs, and other prizes for marketing Target products to their friends and providing the company with feedback—sort of like a street team.

Target asked this group of students to promote Target's Facebook Page but not to tell anyone they were part of the Rounders group. Rosie didn't like that—she thought it sounded unethical—and said so on Target's Facebook Page. Target deleted those messages, and more people started complaining. Target did some damage control and eventually ended up sending Rosie an email agreeing with her and expressing that the idea of staying anonymous was not endorsed by Target.[2]

So when Target said to Amy Jussel just 11 months *after* the Facebook problem that "Target does not participate with nontraditional media outlets," it was untrue as Target clearly had a Facebook Page that it was asking street team members to post to.

What did Target do wrong? Target shouldn't have said two opposite things in different settings about nontraditional media. Either Target didn't participate in social media, or it did participate in social media—but not both! (The company also probably shouldn't have asked students to keep the Rounders promotion a secret. When dealing with public-facing social media, it's generally better to be loudly transparent.)

A Good Example: Domino's Pizza

Now let's look at some good examples of handling criticism. We'll start with Domino's Pizza. A few years ago, Domino's had some major PR trouble. Some Domino's employees posted a video to YouTube where they trash talked their employer and added gross ingredients to the pizzas they were making.[3] The employees were fired, and they later claimed that what they had done in the video was fake. Still, the damage to Domino's was done.

Domino's responded with a YouTube video of its president apologizing,[4] but the response wasn't taken well. President Patrick Doyle was perceived as scripted and less-than-sincere, and he wasn't even looking at the camera. The apology came off as inauthentic.

Domino's has since turned its PR fiasco around. For starters, the company has embraced video and launched a new marketing campaign that tackled the criticism head on. Customer criticism from Twitter is actually included in some of the videos. These videos show Domino's employees listening to their customers and fixing the problems mentioned in the criticisms.

Here's what Rohit Bhargava, author of *Personality Not Included*, says about the Domino's ad campaign: "As someone who has written often about authenticity and personality in business, I love this campaign. It uses real Domino's employees as spokespeople, talks about how much they care about their product (and how hurt they were to hear criticism such as their sauce tasting 'like ketchup'). More importantly, it offers a backstory on how the brand is trying to be different and delivers it in a believable way. The microsite they created even features a live Twitter stream of conversations mentioning their new Pizza, including both good AND bad reviews right on their homepage."[5]

Will it work? A quick news search shows that Domino's profits jumped more than 14 percent after it changed its pizza recipe and pushed it to customers with the reworked marketing campaign.

And Now for the Rest of the Story

Remember that PR agency and the email and Twitter exchange we had? Let's finish that story, because the PR agency turned what started out as a negative experience into an authentic conversation with a positive outcome.

I received one more email and a follow-up phone call from the PR agency that more fully explained the situation. Through those conversations, I learned that the PR agency had a research team that did, in fact, have a small email list of bloggers who focused on library-related topics. The PR person apologized for her lack of research.

She also explained that she didn't send those negative tweets—an intern working for the agency sent them. This intern didn't know about my original email exchange with the agency and thought I was randomly attacking the publisher. The PR person discovered the tweets the intern had sent out and promptly deleted them.

We ended up having a nice chat about small businesses discovering and using social media. The PR agency turned the conversation around from a negative one to a positive one. Here's what the agency did right: The head of the company emailed me personally and listened when I responded. Once she realized what was happening, she apologized and worked to fix the problem.

Getting Coffee in Topeka

There's an amazing coffee shop in Topeka called PT's Coffee that makes the best coffee ever. One Saturday morning, I decided to get some coffee on the way to work. When I arrived at PT's, the coffee shop was busy. The woman at the cash register looked up, said "Just a minute," and then continued doing something behind the counter. The second person working there continued washing a pile of dishes. After the "minute" had stretched to five or six, the dishwasher finally finished his dishes and waited on me.

When I got to work, I tweeted this: "@PTsCoffee—busy at your place this morning. Staff said 'just a sec' then ignored me for 5–6 minutes. Rinsed stuff instead of helping me!"

Very soon after that tweet, I received a reply from @PTsJeff, a cofounder of the company, saying this: "@davidleeking Don't know for sure, very sorry about that. I'll look into it ASAP."

This was a short and sweet reply that came soon after I posted. He acknowledged the problem, apologized promptly, and said he'd look into what was going on. This was good enough for me—he listened.

How Organizations Should Respond to Criticism

If your organization is online, criticism will come. How do you respond appropriately to criticism while still trying to keep that face2face engagement level strong? Here are some ideas to help you through those problems as they occur.

1. *Listen first.* Go and re-read Chapter 5 on listening :-) Really though, you should already be actively listening for customer responses and thoughts. You can't respond if you don't hear anything.

2. *Wait.* After reading a criticism, are you feeling a bit hot under the collar? Irritated? Are you possibly operating without all the facts, like the PR agency intern? You should probably wait to respond until you can do so calmly.

Remember, your goal is customer engagement and fully representing your organization at the same time. Don't say it if your company wouldn't say it.

3. *Admit mistakes and apologize if needed.* If you need to apologize, do so. Quickly. If you were wrong, simply admit it. Admit the mistake, and how you will correct it. Even something as simple as @PTsJeff saying "I'll look into it ASAP" gives customers the feeling that they were at least heard by someone at the organization who cares. That goes a long way.

4. *Be nice.* Sometimes it can be hard to be nice, especially when someone randomly starts attacking your small business or your pet project. Remember, again: Be professional. Business casual, yes—but still represent the organization and not your personal feelings.

5. *Don't always respond.* Sometimes, you don't have to respond. In fact, many times, people who complain about your organization don't necessarily want a response. When I complained about the publisher in Twitter, I wasn't actually looking for a response from someone—I wanted to see if anyone else had received similar emails.

So before you decide to respond, think about your response: Can you add to the conversation? Give more information, a bit more explanation of something, or an apology? If not, you probably don't need to respond.

If the person complaining is a troll, you also shouldn't respond. What's a troll? Wikipedia has a good explanation: "A troll is someone who posts inflammatory, extraneous, or off-topic messages in an online community, such as an online discussion forum, chat room, or blog, with the primary intent of provoking other users into a desired emotional response or of otherwise disrupting normal on-topic discussion."[6]

A good rule of thumb (though it's sometimes hard to do) is this: Don't feed the trolls—meaning, ignore those people completely. Don't respond. If you don't, they'll most likely go away (just like your mom said to do with bullies). If they don't go away, you can block their email addresses, their IP addresses, or their usernames from your website. If trolls are pestering you in a social media site like Twitter or Facebook, you can report them (there's usually a button or link to report bad behavior in social media sites).

6. *Create a commenting policy.* Take a peek at social media policies other organizations use, and adapt them for your business or organization. Don't start deleting comments without one of these! Take another peek at the commenting guidelines created for my library, included in Chapter 2.

7. *Respond in appropriate settings.* Did the criticism start in Facebook? Then respond in Facebook. Was it a comment on your blog? Then respond in the comments to that blog post. Feel free to take the conversation private via email (or even a phone call) if it makes sense—for example, if the criticism started in Twitter. Twitter's great for quick conversations, but replying in a detailed manner doesn't really work in Twitter. An email or a phone call can be more productive.

8. *Redirect.* If the conversation isn't being resolved, or if other people are jumping in and adding their thoughts, you can redirect the conversation. For example, if the conversation started in the comments of a blog post, you can create another blog post with a

full explanation of the situation. Leave a comment on the original blog post that points to the new post with the correct information, and close the comments on the original post.

This serves a couple of purposes. It deflects the trolls, and it also allows a new set of eyes to see the correct information, since it's a new post. That way, your story gets told with a minimum of unneeded rants from trolls.

9. *What if you're correct?* Sometimes, you will be correct, and your critics will be wrong. They might have wrong information or a bad idea, or they simply had a bad day and are being mean. You can respond by correcting the information in a nice way. Share the facts. Many times, that honest response will satisfy critics if they really did want an answer.

10. *Develop a thick skin.* You will need to build a thick skin in online settings. People will criticize and will say nasty things about you and about your company. They will do so anonymously.

Although it's hard, you need to get over it. Realize these people are probably not mad at you personally. They don't even know you! Many times, they are frustrated at something that happened to them concerning your organization. They are venting—they are telling their story.

Can't Please Everyone

Even if you are doing your job really, really well, at some point you are bound to irritate someone. Try to remember this—those critics actually took time out of their busy schedules to say something. Their time is valuable to them, and they chose to spend that time on you and your organization (even though it's in the form of a criticism). That means a lot. Respect their right to have an opinion.

Then, figure out a way to turn their criticism into praise. After all, those people have already demonstrated that they like sharing online. Maybe, just maybe, if you do something they like, they'll share that, too.

Finally, are you wondering "who gets to answer the negative comments when they appear?" I'll cover that in Chapter 10. The answer varies, depending on how you set up your organization, how many staff you have, and how many are assigned to work with social media. It's possible if you are a small business, that person would be you—because you are the *only* employee. If you work at a large organization, you might be able to assign a social media team to handle any critical comments and escalate them as needed.

Endnotes

1. Michael Barbaro, "Target Tells a Blogger to Go Away," NYTimes.com, January 28, 2008, accessed February 14, 2012, www.nytimes.com/2008/01/28/business/media/28target.html.

2. Jackie Crosby, "Bloggers Seeing Red Over Target's Little Secret," StarTribune.com, December 1, 2007, accessed February 14, 2012, www.startribune.com/business/11987331.html.

3. Rebecca Lieb, "Domino's Social Media Mess," Econsultancy, April 14, 2009, accessed February 14, 2012, www.econsultancy.com/us/blog/3673-dominos-social-media-mess-3.

4. Graham Charlton, "Is Domino's YouTube Response Enough?" Econsultancy, April 16, 2009, accessed February 14, 2012, www.econsultancy.com/us/blog/3684-is-dominos-youtube-response-enough.

5. Rohit Bhargava, "Can Domino's Turn Around Their Cardboard Reputation?" Influential Marketing Blog, January 19, 2010, accessed February 14, 2012, www.rohitbhargava.typepad.com/weblog/2010/01/can-dominos-turn-around-their-cardboard-reputation.html.

6. "Troll (Internet)," Wikipedia, accessed February 14, 2012, secure.wikimedia.org/wikipedia/en/wiki/Troll_(Internet).

CHAPTER
10

Where and How to Begin

I hope you have learned a lot in the previous chapters about how to create and sustain engaged face2face connections with customers and potential customers. In these last few chapters, we will focus on the next steps. How do you begin showing your organizational "human side" on a corporate blog? How do you start creating and maintaining online, personalized invitations to connect to your organization's Facebook account? Where do you begin?

This chapter will answer those questions, Chapter 11 will show you how to measure results, and Chapter 12 will provide an example of a small business that is just starting out.

This chapter focuses on:

- Asking

- Setting goals

- Creating strategy
- Doing the work

Let's get started!

Asking

Often, the best place to start asking questions is with your current customers, potential customers, and people in close proximity to your business. Ask them questions like:

- What they want you to do
- How they'd like to connect with you
- If they like receiving deals via Facebook or Twitter
- How you can better serve them as they connect with you— with your organization, as they use your services, etc.
- What they like or don't like about your new service or product

Those questions should get you started. How should you ask? There are multiple ways to ask, including person-to-person, focus groups, and surveys.

Person-to-Person

These days, person-to-person doesn't necessarily mean being physically present. Communicating person-to-person can mean via email, text message, IM, or a direct message in Twitter. But it's still directed at a single individual who you know in some context—hence, person-to-person.

Person-to-person asking can actually be as simple as cornering your friends and relatives. Ask them if they like friending organizations online. Depending on the type of organization you have, that could be useful information.

You can also, of course, focus on your customers. Look for active customers—the ones you already recognize, who are in your store or using your services. Online, look for similar types of people—people who are already interacting in some way with you. They're the ones who frequently Like one of your status updates on Facebook or already leave comments there. Maybe they're in the habit of retweeting your Twitter posts. These are the people you recognize in some way.

These people are already interacting with your organization, though you might not have thought about it in that way. They're already engaged.

Ask them things like:

- Do you read blogs?

- Do you leave comments online?

- Do you participate in surveys?

- Do you like receiving coupons via Facebook?

- Do you ever have a question about our organization but don't want to make a phone call?

- How do you want to connect with us?

- Why do you want to connect with us?

Then, once you have made a semi-direct connection with these people, continue asking them questions. Ask things like: Did you use our service? How was it? Anyone buy that new item? If so, what do you think? For TSCPL, we might ask "What was the last book you checked out, did you like it, and why?" Questions will also jumpstart interactions between your organization and your customers—you will be creating and maintaining face2face connections.

Here's the deal: If those people interact with you on less serious, short-form questions, you have a better chance of those same customers and contacts being willing to answer longer-form questions when you need a deeper level of input or direction for your organization.

Focus Groups

A focus group is a small group of people you gather together to participate in a guided discussion about a particular product or service before it launches or to provide ongoing feedback about your organization. This simple concept can be very powerful.

TSCPL has used focus groups to gather information before we start a website redesign. We'll hold two to four focus group sessions, with five to 10 people participating in each group. During each focus group session, we will ask questions about our website such as:

- What do you like most about the website?

- What do you not like?

- What doesn't make sense?

- What are your favorite websites to visit?

- What would you like to do here but can't?

The answers we receive during the sessions are invaluable to us. We refer back to them during our redesign process.

We look for those active customers mentioned earlier to be our focus group participants. These are active users of our services. Online, we look for frequent Facebook users—Facebook followers who are already actively using the tools (Facebook) and the service (our library). This can be a great way to find people already willing to interact with your organization. If they like commenting on your Facebook status updates, perhaps they'd also be willing to help out in another setting.

Remember, in a focus group setting, you're not really looking for specific information. You're looking for reactions and for participants' thoughts about whatever it is you ask.

Glenn David Blank, an associate professor of computer science at Lehigh University, says to concentrate on these types of results from your focus group:[1]

- Gathering opinions, beliefs, and attitudes about issues of interest to your organization

- Testing your assumptions

- Encouraging discussion about a particular topic

- Building excitement from spontaneous combination of participants' comments

- Providing an opportunity to learn more about a topic or issue

Gather this type of information, and you are well on your way to figuring out how to interact with your customers.

Surveys

Surveys are another way to poll relatively active customers and ask for their help in developing and guiding your organization to the next level. Surveys are an easy way to gather information about specific things. Ask something specific, with simple multiple choice or yes/no answers. Make it quick and simple to increase your chances that customers will complete the survey.

Surveying people used to be a pretty time-consuming activity. Remember those part-time market research jobs at the local mall, where people stand around for hours, looking for specific types of people to pester into answering a few questions? Thankfully, we don't have to do that anymore. You can easily direct people to fill out short surveys on your website or on your Facebook Page.

Keep your survey short. I wouldn't advise asking more than 10 questions. The survey should take no longer than five minutes to complete. People generally don't want to answer 100 time-consuming, detailed survey questions. If it feels like a test, you have definitely lost people. If the survey is short and it seems like you are asking for opinions, you have a greater chance of a good response.

With surveys, you are looking for answers to specific questions and for trends. Here's what Survey Monkey, a popular online survey tool, suggests about what to avoid while asking survey questions:[2]

- Avoid leading questions: You don't want to lead your respondents into answering a certain way based on the wording of the questions.

- Avoid loaded questions: These types of questions work through emotionally charged items like words, stereotypes, and so on. This too can push respondents toward a specific answer choice.

- Avoid built-in assumptions: You shouldn't ask questions that assume the respondents are familiar with the specifics of it. Include details or additional information if necessary.

- Avoid jargon—use simple language: You should try to use words that are direct and familiar to the respondents. Try not to use jargon or technical concepts.

- Avoid double negatives or double-barreled questions:
  Double-barreled questions split questions into more than
  one part, idea, or meaning. The answer choice for each
  part might have separate meanings to the ideas
  presented within one question.

Setting Goals

After asking, the next most important step to take is to start setting
goals. Every project needs goals: business-facing goals and people-
facing goals. You'll definitely have business-facing goals, like earn-
ing more profit or helping more people. But you also need goals
focused on creating and sustaining ways to connect with your customers—ways to be consistently human in your organization's
interactions with its customers.

Goals for Facebook might include always using business casual
language. Maybe you'll have a practical goal of posting five status
updates a week. Those status updates might focus on these ideas:

- Sharing thoughts about a product or your organization's
  industry

- Sharing links to new posts on your organization's blog or
  videos of how to get value out of a new service

- Responding to comments and replies

- Answering questions as they appear

A major goal for your organization might be to expand your
reach in your customer community. At TSCPL, this means getting
to know our library customers. To do that, we invite them to friend
us in social networks. A large number of people in Topeka and
Shawnee County use Facebook and to a lesser extent Twitter.

Because of that, we are sure to actively nurture community in those networks. It's a great way to connect to our library customers. We make an effort to have conversations with our customers in those settings, just like we do in our building and out in the community. This may encourage more library card holders in the process.

If you're a business or organization, this might be a way to sell more, sign more people up, and so on—by introducing people to your services, and then by starting, sustaining, and participating in conversations that take place about those services and the issues surrounding them.

Creating Strategy

Now you have four to five goals surrounding how to create and sustain face2face connections with your customers by using online networks. What's next? You need to create strategies that help your organization meet those goals.

Creating strategy is simply creating steps that help you get to your end result. This is much like planning a vacation. First you figure out where you want to visit (the goal), and then you figure out all the details (the strategy) that will get you to that relaxing beach!

Here's an example. Say your goal is to get more Facebook friends. (Facebook actually calls it Likes. YouTube calls them subscribers, and Twitter calls them followers. I'm using the general term *friends* to describe these connections.) To meet that goal, your strategy might look like this:

- Friend organizations in your service area that have a Facebook presence. Look for partner organizations— preferably partner organizations with a good dose of activity on their Facebook Wall.

- Start conversations with those organizations on their Facebook Pages. If there is a status update, comment on it. Hopefully, other people will comment too and start a conversation.

- On your own Facebook Page, simply ask for more friends!

You can also ask for friends in other ways. For example, if you hold an event, take the first two minutes to tell people about your Facebook Page. Then ask participants to friend your organization.

The Work

You'll also need to figure out who does the work of determining strategy. In our Facebook example, who runs the Facebook Page? Who checks out and friends people? Who answers questions and responds to comments? That's real work that needs to be done.

Instead of asking for volunteers and crossing your fingers, be sure to assign responsibilities and set timelines and due dates. This way, you'll be able to measure progress toward your goal and know if the work was done well and in a timely fashion.

What Success Looks Like

How does one measure success? Let's refer back to our Facebook goal of getting more friends. Success with that goal might be a couple of things. Success, obviously, could mean seeing an increase in Facebook friends, which is easy to count and track. In fact, Facebook Pages can send out a weekly email showing the number of friends gained each week, so growth can be monitored (Figure 10.1). You can also check out Facebook Insights for your Facebook Page and monitor growth over a longer period of time.

Success for this goal could also mean an increase in awareness of your organization's products or services. Maybe because you

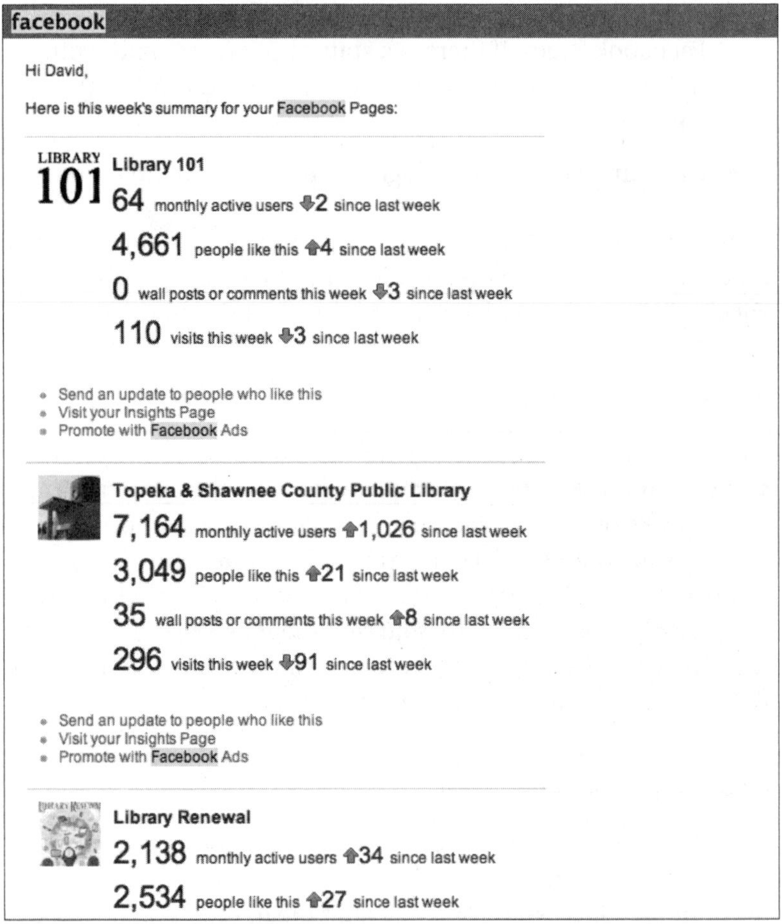

facebook

Hi David,

Here is this week's summary for your Facebook Pages:

LIBRARY 101

Library 101

64 monthly active users ⇩2 since last week

4,661 people like this ⇧4 since last week

0 wall posts or comments this week ⇩3 since last week

110 visits this week ⇩3 since last week

- Send an update to people who like this
- Visit your Insights Page
- Promote with Facebook Ads

Topeka & Shawnee County Public Library

7,164 monthly active users ⇧1,026 since last week

3,049 people like this ⇧21 since last week

35 wall posts or comments this week ⇧8 since last week

296 visits this week ⇩91 since last week

- Send an update to people who like this
- Visit your Insights Page
- Promote with Facebook Ads

Library Renewal

2,138 monthly active users ⇧34 since last week

2,534 people like this ⇧27 since last week

Figure 10.1 Weekly Facebook Pages summary email

started interacting with people and other organizations via a Facebook Page, those partner organizations mentioned you or your services more regularly than they used to. Increased mentions can potentially be tracked over time. One way to do that would be to set up an alerts feed or subscribe to responders'

Facebook Pages or Twitter feeds, and then keep track of mentions from other organizations.

Success might mean an increase in numbers elsewhere. Maybe more people attended an event because they discovered it through Facebook. To measure that, you'd need to ask how people heard about the event. You can ask and take a quick show of hands, or you might pass out a response form.

Maybe, more people visited your business or used your service because they read about it on Facebook. Again, this is easily discoverable by simply asking how people found out about your organization.

What to Do Next

Your final strategy is to figure out what to do next. Hopefully, you will meet that first set of goals. And honestly, even if those goals didn't fully succeed, you will need to regroup and figure out the next steps to take anyway.

Doing the Work

At this point, you are doing great. You have set some reachable goals for your organization, and you have multiple strategies to reach those goals. You have figured out ways to listen. You know how to connect to your customers.

What's next? Actually starting. And I'm not being funny here. I know of more than one organization that has created detailed plans for a project or has created a great strategic planning document ... only to put it in a binder and place it on a shelf, where it then gathers dust until the next strategic planning session a couple of years later.

Want to get those plans accomplished? The best way, many times, is to jump in with both feet and just start. Then, adjust as needed. If you find that the work was too much for one person and you have the resources, add another person to the project. If you find you're getting less activity than anticipated, trim down. Also adjust for success. Most likely, if you focus on the goals and the strategy you created, you will have thought through many of the major obstacles you might face, so those are more easily navigated.

Using Real, Live Employees

It is very important that your organization has adequate staffing to sustain face2face goals. Being human online takes time. It's very similar to connecting with customers in a store setting or at an event. Connecting with customers in person takes time and resources, possibly even training for the floor staff.

Guess what? It's the same thing online. It will take real, live, full-time staff to interact with your customers online. These employees will need to have excellent customer service and communication skills—not just those 20th-century "written and oral" communication skills asked for in job ads. Twenty-first century communication skills still involve both written and spoken forms, just with a new twist on the modern web. Staff need to know how to write for the web. They need to know how to write in a business casual, inverted pyramid style. They need to know how to connect with people using a status update box that might only provide 140 characters.

Staff doing these jobs should also be familiar with multiple social networks and will need to enjoy connecting with strangers in those settings. This advice works for large and small organizations. If you have the luxury of assigning a team of staff to social media, great! Do it, and let them get started. It's generally better to have your actual staff do the work of social media—after all, "social media" is nothing more than talking with your customers. Who knows your customers best—an outside social media marketing firm, or your staff?

If you are a small organization, or even a team of one or two people, you face some unique challenges—you have to do all the work. Schedule times for focus on customer relationship building through social media. For example, set aside 15 minutes every morning to interact with customers on Twitter or Facebook. Post some pictures to Flickr or a quick video to YouTube. If you make it a scheduled priority, you will find time for it.

Do these things and you are well on your way to improving your face2face game.

Endnotes

1. Glenn David Blank, "Conducting a Focus Group," accessed February 14, 2012, www.cse.lehigh.edu/~glennb/mm/FocusGroups.htm.

2. "Writing Survey Questions: Tips for Writing Effective and Relevant Survey Questions," Survey Monkey, accessed February 14, 2012, help.surveymonkey.com/app/answers/detail/a_id/134/~/tips-for-writing-effective-and-relevant-survey-questions.

Measuring Success

In the previous chapter, I briefly mentioned measurement. In this chapter, let's focus more specifically on measurement and analytics tools, and answer some questions, including:

- Why measure?

- What can be measured?

- How do we measure?

Why You Need to Measure

First, let's tackle this question: Why should you measure? Does it really matter if you know that 20 more people friended you in

Twitter last week, or which of your Facebook status updates are the most popular?

Well ... yes and no. Yes, it does matter—when you measure the things you actually care about. This assumes that your organization or business has actually created some short- and long-term goals and that you have strategies in place to meet those goals. If that's the case, then yes, measurement is important. There are probably ways to match your organization's goals with social media strategies that can help reach those goals. Those social media strategies can be measured and monitored to watch for trends and growth, so you know if you are reaching your goals.

And, no, it doesn't matter. With social media, it's very easy to focus on the wrong benchmarks. If your goal is to sell more widgets, measuring the number of Facebook Page Likes you receive isn't necessarily going to sell more widgets. But if you measure the amount of engagement created by a Facebook post discussing your next widget sale, and then you measure click-throughs and conversion rates from that particular post to an actual sale, that *is* useful and will help grow your business.

See the difference? Analytics are all about strategy. First, figure out your organization's goals, and then figure out the right tools to use to help you reach those goals. Once that's done, then you can start monitoring analytics (assuming the social media tools you picked have something to measure) to watch for trends and growth over time.

What to Measure

What should you measure? There are a lot of social media sites out there, and I've talked about a number of the most important ones. Each of those sites has things that can be measured—for instance, the number of friends or Likes, demographics, the number of comments, the number of views, and external referrers.

Let's look at some of the more popular tools mentioned in this book, and see what types of data and interactions can be measured.

Facebook

Facebook has integrated analytics into Facebook Pages by way of Facebook Insights. Insights can monitor almost 20 things, all potentially useful, depending on your organization's goals. Facebook Insights has five tabs: Overview, Likes, Reach, Talking About This, and Check-Ins. Figure 11.1 shows what you can find on the Overview tab.

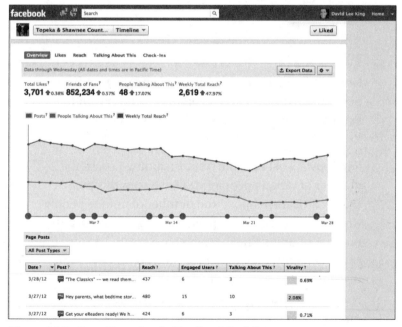

Figure 11.1   Page Overview in Facebook Insights

Overview

Overview is the main summary page of Insights and provides all of the most important analytics, broken into the following:

- Numbers: The number of Total Likes (the number of unique people who liked your Page), Friends of Fans (the number of unique people who were friends of people who like your Page), People Talking About This (the number of unique people who have created a Story about your Page; a Story is created when someone Likes your page, Likes or comments on your post, and mentions your Page, etc.), and Weekly Total Reach (the number of unique people who have seen any content associated with your page, including ads or sponsored Stories that point to your Page).

- Graph: Display of the bubbles showing the number of posts made during a day, overlapping those with the People Talking About This and Weekly Total Reach numbers.

- Page posts: Post-specific stats, including Reach (the number of unique people who have seen this post), Engaged Users per post (the number of unique people who have clicked on the post), Talking About This (the number of unique people who have created a Story from your Page post, including Likes and comments), and Virality (the percentage of people who have created a Story from your Page post out of the total number of unique people who have seen it).

Likes

The Likes tab is divided into three sections:

- Gender and Age: Graph of the gender and age of people who have Liked your Page providing a percentage of male/female users and showing age ranges (13–17, 18–24, 25–34, 35–44, 45–54, and 55+).

- Countries, Cities, and Languages: The top seven countries, cities, and languages of people who have Liked your Page, including a More button you can click to get an expanded list.

- Where Your Likes Came From: Where Likes within Facebook came from, including Facebook Recommendations, On Page, Mobile, Timeline, Like Box and Like Button, Admin Invite, Page Browser, Ticker, Search Results, and On Hover.

Reach

Reach focuses on who your Facebook Page is reaching, including Gender and Age and Countries, Cities, and Languages, as well as the following:

- How You Reached People: Graph showing where views came from and a bar graph displaying the number of times people saw your posts.

- Visits to Your Page: Visits broken down in three different ways: Page views (shows page views and unique pages views for the current month), Total Tab views (a breakdown of Page views by tab, including the Wall, the Timeline, Events, etc.), and External Referrers (a list of the top referring external domains sending traffic to your Page, with data for the current month).

Talking About This

The Talking About This section includes Gender and Age and Countries, Cities, and Languages, as well as the following:

- How People Are Talking About Your Page: Graph showing the number of unique people who created a story about your Page and a Viral Reach graph showing the number of unique people who saw a Story published by a friend about your Page.

Check-Ins

The Check-Ins section provides data on the number of people who have checked-in at your location using Facebook's location-based check-in feature. Gender and Age (demographic data only available when more than 30 people check in during the date range shown) and Countries, Cities, and Languages (data only available when more than 30 people check in during the date range shown) are included, as well as the following:

- How People Check In at Your Place: The number of people checking in through Facebook's website and via a mobile device.

Flickr

Flickr provides solid statistics for Flickr Pro accounts (approximately $25 per year to set up a Pro account) that focus on views and activity surrounding your Flickr photos. Statistics include the following:

- Daily aggregate views: A graph that plots the number of views, comments, and favorites for all your photos.

- View counts: The number of views your account receives on photos and videos, your photostream, sets, collections, and galleries. These numbers are broken into Today, Yesterday, and All Time.

- Most viewed photos and videos: The number of views, comments, and favorites for your most popular photos. Numbers for Today, Yesterday, and All Time (if you click the All Photos and Videos link) are provided.

- Referrers: The top external domains visiting your photos. The number of visits for Today and Yesterday are given.

- Breakdown of your photos and videos: For your account, the number of photos, how many are public/private, how many are tagged/not tagged, how many in sets, etc.

YouTube

YouTube provides a very thorough Insight section for every YouTube account. It includes the following results (Figure 11.2):

- Summary: A general overview for the last month. It includes views per day, top videos, basic demographics, and a popularity world map showing how popular your videos are relative to those of other uploaders.

- Views: The total number of video views made in a day; daily and weekly numbers, as well as those for the last month; and the 10 most popular videos. A percent of total views is given.

- Discovery: Insight into how people find your videos, which is divided into two sections:

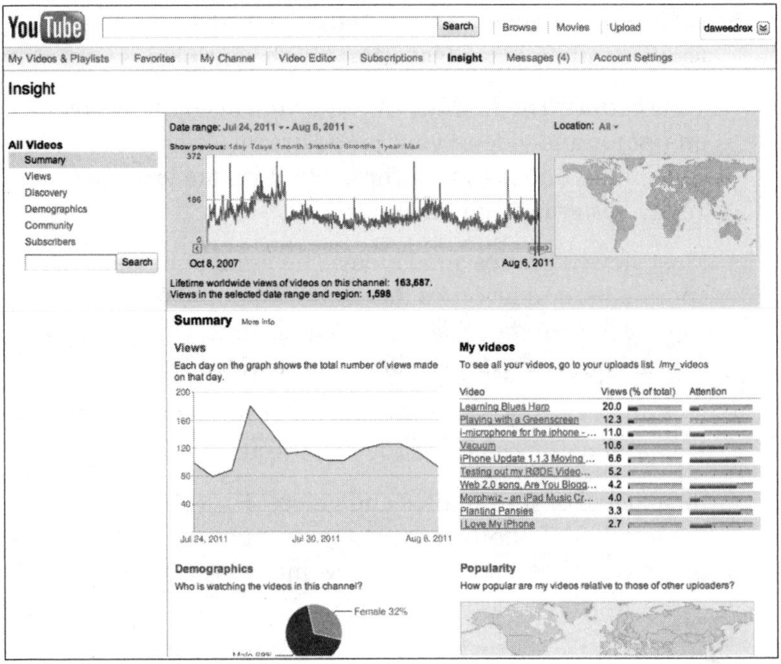

Figure 11.2   YouTube Insight results page

- Links followed to this video: A percentage of total views, and the type of link. Ten link types are given, including YouTube-related video, embedded player, mobile devices, external websites, and Google Search.

- Location of player when viewed: List includes the YouTube watch page, embedded player on other websites, mobile devices, and YouTube channel page.

• Demographics: An age and gender breakdown. A male/female percentage is provided, and age is broken into 13–17, 18–24, 25–34, 35–44, 45–54, 55–64, and 65+.

- Community: Percentages for the number of times people share, rate, favorite, or comment on a video within YouTube.

- Subscribers: The number of people currently subscribed to your YouTube channel.

Twitter

Twitter analytics are harder to find because you either have to count them manually or use a third-party product. According to Mashable, Twitter is working on an analytics product and has released it for beta testing to "a select group of users."[1] So it is possible that by the time you are reading this, Twitter will have built-in analytics. Let's hope so because that would make Twitter statistics much easier to track. Until then, there are two ways to track things: manually and through third-party tools.

Manually

You can track some things manually in Twitter. It's easy enough to visit your Twitter profile page on a regular basis and keep track of the number of tweets sent, the number of followers and the number of people you are following, and how many times someone "Lists" you. You can drop that number into a spreadsheet, and then track it once a month to show growth over time.

Third-Party Tools

There are many third-party Twitter tools that provide statistics; some cost thousands of dollars per month, and some are free. Each of them track slightly different things or track the same statistic in slightly different ways. Two examples of solid free tools for tracking some basic Twitter statistics are:

- Twitter Counter (www.twittercounter.com): Twitter Counter provides basic statistics for the number of followers, the number of people you follow, the number of tweets you publish, and a mixed graph showing the number of tweets published and the number of followers on a given day. Statistics are given for day, week, month, and 3- and 6-month intervals. Twitter Counter also provides a weekly email showing you how many new followers your Twitter account gained and will predict the amount of future followers you will gain over time.

- TweetStats (www.tweetstats.com): Currently, there's a bit of a wait time issue with TweetStats. For example, in one instance, I was #154 in line to have my statistics processed, and it took about an hour for my statistics to display. Once that happens, a TweetStats user will see similar statistics to Twitter Counter, plus some other useful analytics. Statistics provided include the number of tweets sent, the time of day you tweet, what day of the week you send tweets, who you reply to, who you retweet, and what interface you use to tweet.

Foursquare

Foursquare provides some interesting statistics on check-ins (Figure 11.3):

- All-time check-ins: The total number of check-ins for your venue. The current mayor is also shown.

- Venue stats: Total check-ins, average check-ins per day, unique and new visitors, social reach (if the check-in was sent to Twitter or Facebook), a time breakdown by hour for check-ins, and a gender and age breakdown. Data can

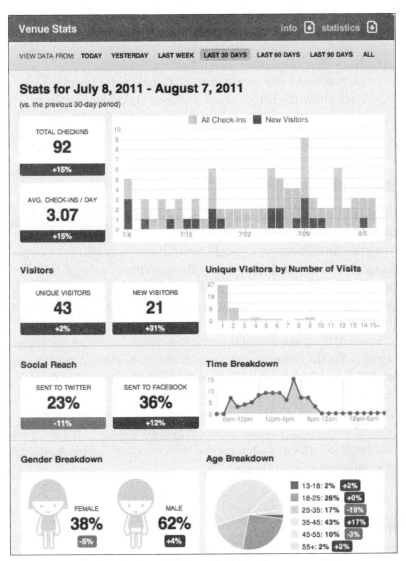

Figure 11.3   Foursquare Analytics results page

be displayed for Today, Yesterday, Last Week, Last 30 Days, Last 60 Days, and All.

- Top visitors and most recent visitors: A venue's top visitors and most recent visitors, found under People. Each show 10 visitors, the number of check-ins they have done at the venue, and their Twitter addresses, if they have one linked to their Foursquare accounts.

Blogs and Websites

Blogs and websites can use a variety of web analytics reporting tools. One great tool that also happens to be free is Google Analytics. Just go to www.google.com/analytics to sign up. Google Analytics is easy to install (just add a snippet of code into the header or footer of your website after your account is created). Once installed, Google Analytics keeps track of some very in-depth information for your website.

Some of the more useful information tracked includes the number of visits, the bounce rate (the percentage of visitors to your site who "bounce" away, or visit, another website immediately after visiting your site), average time spent on your site, popular pages or blog posts, types of browsing devices used (especially useful for sites interested in mobile technology), and more. This list just touches the surface of what can be tracked using Google Analytics or similar analytics software.

How to Measure

Each of the tools I've mentioned have different options for reporting, but the two main ways to report are via scheduled reports and manually.

Some of the tools send out a weekly or monthly email that includes the summary overview statistics provided on the site's statistics or insights pages. Facebook and Tweet Counter both do this, for example. Google Analytics can be set up to email daily, weekly, monthly, or quarterly analytics reports.

For the other tools, one easy way to track usage and trends over time is to set a reminder up in your calendar and create a simple spreadsheet to store statistics. Then, every month, visit the statistics pages of the social media tools you're interested in tracking and record the new numbers.

Track Those Stats

Either way you track, analytics provide great insight into what's happening on your website, on your social media sites, and with your content. Keep track of them, and you'll start getting a handle on what types of content your customers respond to best, the time of day they generally like to connect with you and your organization, and the average age range of your social-media-savvy customers.

This information can definitely be useful to the growth of your company!

Endnote

1. Adam Ostrow, "Twitter's Official Analytics Product Has Arrived," Mashable, November 17, 2010, accessed February 14, 2012, mashable.com/2010/11/17/ twitter-analytics.

CHAPTER 12

Applying What We've Learned

Whether you've read every chapter or simply skipped to this one, welcome to The Last Chapter!

This chapter is the "application" chapter. We are going to take some of what we've learned throughout this book and apply it to a business setting to see how making face2face connections works in the real world.

To do that, let's pretend we have a small business. We'll create a lovely little coffee shop named Clyde's Café. Clyde's sells coffee and has cool, talented baristas who make leaf designs in the foam of your lattes. The café also sells tea, pastries, and the usual coffee-related gadgets and gizmos, like personal espresso-making gear and T-shirts.

Clyde's Café is a new business and the owner wants to connect with customers online. The owner, Clyde Smith, has a passion for coffee, is pretty outgoing, loves people, and has always wanted to start his own business with his wife. And now they own a small coffee shop with five employees, plus themselves. They really believe in the power of community, since they've seen it in action in their own lives many times. They also believe in the power of the web and want to try to extend their reach to their city's local online community.

Clyde is starting from scratch, just like many small business owners. He doesn't know much about the web and never really had a need or the desire to learn. But now he has both. How should Clyde make the jump into the world of the social web?

Listening

Clyde's first step would be to start listening, just like we learned to do in Chapter 5. Clyde should also start by setting up a Twitter account, so it's ready when he starts responding. But at first, Clyde should primarily listen, and he can do this using Twitter Search. Clyde can set up some advanced searches for topics of interest to his business, like *coffee, breakfast, bagel,* or even *morning.* While creating those searches, Clyde can also localize them to find only the tweets from people living in his city by using the Near: operator (or by adding the name and state of his city in the "Near this place" box on the Twitter Search Advanced Search page).

Then Clyde can subscribe to those searches by clicking the Save This Search button in Twitter. To revisit that search (once Clyde logs in to Twitter), he can find Saved Searches on the main page, right by Timeline, @Mentions, Retweets, and Lists. Or Clyde could use other tools to monitor those searches, like HootSuite or TweetDeck. Both tools place each Twitter feed, mention, and search in separate columns, and many people find the multicolumn view of Twitter to be easier to follow. Instead of trying to follow all Twitter updates in separate tabs at Twitter.com, a multicolumn view allows you to quickly see mentions, direct messages, or search results as they appear.

Either way, once those searches are created, Clyde has one easy job to do: Listen. Just by reading, he can simply monitor what people in his area—his potential customers—are saying about those topics. Once Clyde gets familiar with the banter taking place, if he starts to notice some Twitter names that appear often, he can start friending them. But at this stage, his primary job is to find out who that morning/afternoon/evening coffee crowd is and what they're doing.

Sharing

The next step for Clyde, after he gets a feel for Twitter and the topics he's monitoring, is to start following people and to start sharing. What should he share? Some ideas of things to share include the obvious—that there's a new coffee shop in town. He could share that their coffee is better than everyone else's and why. If there is something unique about their café, Clyde should share that, too.

Clyde should also revisit those saved searches at this point and start adding to the conversations taking place. He needs to follow people and join in those conversations. Since Clyde has been monitoring conversations and is knowledgeable about the topic, he should have good information to add.

For example, if someone comments about a certain flavor of coffee, Clyde can probably join in on that conversation. If someone asks a question about coffeemakers, I'll bet Clyde can answer that question. While answering questions and conversing, Clyde shouldn't be actively trying to sell his business. No mentions of the coffee shop, coupons, or other promotions. People can find that information by clicking through to Clyde's Twitter profile page (which should point to his café's website). If done right, people will become interested in Clyde's business because he seems helpful and likable through how he acts on Twitter.

Using Social Media Tools

At this point, Clyde should also start setting up accounts in other social media tools. Following is a rundown of the useful tools Clyde should think about joining or creating for his business and how he might use them.

Twitter

Clyde has already been using Twitter to connect and to answer questions, and that's a perfect use for Twitter for an organization. Clyde can also start sharing additional information, like fun things customers say or new coffee flavors. Twitter will also continue to be a place to answer questions and respond to comments.

Website and Blog

Clyde can check out other café websites for inspiration and then create his own site. On his site, he needs to be sure to include all the usual who, what, why, when, where, and how information. Clyde can also create a "What's Happening at Clyde's" blog and add elements such as a newsletter telling patrons what's happening this week at the café. This is a great place to start sharing milestones. For Clyde, some milestones could be things like moving in, painting, remodeling, or even that new, cool "Clyde's Café" coffee mugs have arrived. Those blog posts can be funneled into Twitter and Facebook via third-party tools like Twitterfeed (or by the good ole manual copy/paste).

Clyde can also use his website and blog for out-in-the-community conversations. He can share when he gets a special type of coffee in the store (and describe what it tastes like) or introduce new staff with a picture or a video.

Facebook Page

Facebook can be used in a similar way to Twitter: for sharing and conversations. Clyde will probably have a different audience here than on his Twitter account, since 51 percent of Americans age 13 and older use Facebook, and a much smaller percentage of people use Twitter.

(So why did Clyde start with Twitter? Twitter users tend to be the most active social media users and tend to be media creators, working in TV, radio, newspaper, and marketing. They are really good people for Clyde to know, and being active on Twitter can lead to marketing or promotional opportunities down the road. This is basic networking with your most active social audience.)

YouTube

Clyde could even create some short videos and share those. For example, why not create a video of Clyde unboxing the new espresso machine? The video could then show Clyde turning it on and show Clyde and his wife tasting a cup of the brew from the new machine. That video can be uploaded to YouTube, and then embedded onto the café's blog. It can also be uploaded to Facebook or embedded there as a Wall post. It can also be shared via Twitter in a variety of ways.

For his café, Clyde can make a day-in-the-life video once in a while—a what's happening at the store or a funny stories video. That will help make the store seem interesting, fun, and inviting.

Flickr

Flickr can be used in the same way as YouTube. Clyde can take photos of the café, of customers drinking coffee, of the staff, and of the storefront, and then upload the photos to Flickr. Flickr allows him to easily use those photos on the blog and on the website, and post them to Facebook and Twitter, where he can let people comment on them.

For both video and still images, the camera can capture new products, new mugs, rearrangements, and new staff. The same holds true with the video camera. Make sure the videos go on YouTube and Facebook, and be sure to upload the photos to Flickr and Facebook.

Location-Based Tools

Since Clyde is located in a midsized city, he can also set up a location service like Foursquare. This allows people to check in to his place and share it with their friends. Clyde is even thinking about giving people 10 percent off when they show staff they checked in or if they checked in and shared that check-in with their friends.

Niche Social Networks

In Clyde's case, since he owns a café, he should pay close attention to Yelp and similar services that allow users to comment on their experiences with local businesses. Yelp (www.yelp.com) is a social network set up for people to review businesses—including restaurants and cafés, like Clyde's. A business can't change or delete reviews people leave, but they can set up an official "business account" in Yelp and respond to reviews, message customers, and even create Yelp Deals and events.

Doing the Work

In Clyde's case, there are two owners, five employees ... and a whole lot of social media work that needs to be done! Who "does the work" will vary by organization. In some cases, the owner or a manager might do it. In other cases, a part-time employee might be assigned to monitor social media.

My suggestion is to divide the work. One person can pretty easily create one or two blog posts a week, and that shouldn't take more than 30 minutes or so. Have a camera or video camera handy, and employees can take photos or videos when the moment strikes. It might work to actually assign these tasks. For example, each week someone might be assigned to take photos or videos of interesting things going on in the café. If you carry a smartphone with those capabilities, you'll have a camera in your pocket all the time, so you'll be ready.

Twitter and Facebook can be handled on an as-needed basis. Set them up and turn on alerts to your smartphone. This way, when someone mentions you in a comment or question, you'll see it immediately and can respond quickly.

Empowering Staff

If Clyde wants his employees to share the social media workload, he needs to first clearly explain to them what his standards and expectations are. Certainly let them be themselves, but remember what I've said throughout: They should be personable, they should be business casual, and they should remember who they're representing (i.e., Clyde's Café).

Once trained, Clyde can allow staff to share what's going on, if it's a slow time at the shop. He can empower staff to tweet funny things that happen, share an inspiring story, or assign them to take photographs of a new display they set up and have them post the photos to Facebook. Yes, this means that Clyde will need to set up a computer in the back room or provide a store iPhone. This is probably a small price to pay for creating community connections that can potentially make the difference in whether his shop succeeds or fails.

Creating Strategy and Goals

So far, Clyde has set up some social media tools that help monitor what his customers are saying about him and about his industry, and he's set up some other tools to help him share Clyde's Café with his customers. In the process, he has started to create some loose strategies and goals around his social media usage, probably resembling this: answer questions, make customers happy, send out coupons, and share what's going on at Clyde's with the world.

Those are great goals to have, for starters. However, as Clyde's business grows, and as Clyde's use of social media for his business grows, he will need to create some short- and long-term goals for social media, and figure out some strategies that will help meet those goals.

What might Clyde's goals look like? Instead of creating separate social media goals, look at the company or organization's goals, and then try to help meet those organizational goals via social media tools.

Let's do that for Clyde. In Clyde's case, he has some challenging but attainable goals, including:

- Get early-morning business customers.

- Get nighttime customers: He's located downtown, and there's a revitalization project going on that he supports. So he wants to help draw people to the downtown area after work, too.

- Sell coffee, obviously: Clyde wants to introduce his city to what he considers the best coffee in the world.

- Set the mood: Clyde wants to connect with the creatives in town, so creating the right ambiance is important.

How can social media further these goals? Friending the downtown workers on Facebook and Twitter and holding conversations with them will help get Clyde's foot in the door for the morning business crowd. Once that is accomplished, offering grand-opening sales and coupons (and actually having tasty coffee) will help. Creating tweetups, social media breakfasts, and other informal meetings that social media users attend is another way to attract those customers to Clyde's.

Other ideas for Clyde: Why not offer to hang up local artist's works in the café, and then connect with the city's monthly artwalk? Take photos of new art (with the artist's permission), dump those photos to Flickr, and tweet the links out a couple days before the event. Host book signings with local authors. Connect with local poets, bands, or musicians on Facebook or Twitter, and let them be his Friday evening entertainment.

For the "best coffee in the world" part, Clyde will need to do some serious sharing—via YouTube and his blog—on why he thinks his coffee is the best. And the best way to do that is to talk with his customers and share what they say. When a customer tweets out something positive, Clyde can retweet it and post the tweet on his blog. His staff can create videos of customers sharing what they like about the coffee. Doing this right can help create buzz around the coffee and around Clyde's Café, and help him start meeting those goals.

Measuring Success

Clyde has some great goals, has some strategies to help meet them, and has a bunch of social media accounts. How will he know if he is on the right track? On the social media end of things, there's a variety of ways to measure success, including:

- Number of friends: The growth of people friending you over time. If people are friending your business, you are doing something right. If not, you need to find out why not (by asking your customers).

- Number of Likes: How many people Liked your status update in Facebook. This is a gauge of interest in what you said. Over time, look through your top Likes (on the Overview page in Facebook Insights) and for patterns. Did you do something different on those posts? Are there certain hot topics? If you see a pattern, continue to provide that type of content.

- Number of conversations: Includes Twitter mentions and Facebook, blog, YouTube, and Flickr comments. Count them, but more importantly, look for trends. Why do people comment more on some posts? Look for patterns and continue to do those things.

- Total monthly views/visits/impressions: A measure of how many people saw a blog post, a Facebook status update, a YouTube video, or a Flickr post. It's a gauge of popularity and interest in your content (and therefore your organization). Again, look for trends, figure out what people like, and repeat.

- External referrers: Who points to your website or Facebook Page from other websites. It potentially identifies some of your most loyal customers.

- Virality: The ratio of total Likes and comments on a status update over the total number of times the status update was seen. This is Facebook-specific. It looks at impressions, Likes, and comments, and provides a percentage. It's one of the few built-in gauges of engagement that I've seen from a social network. Figure out what you did on those posts, and do more of it.

- Demographics: Age range of the viewers and a male/female breakdown. YouTube and Facebook both show these demographics. This is a handy gauge to see if your content is reaching your target audience. If so, congrats—keep it up! If not, look through your content, and adjust accordingly.

- Conversion rate: The ratio of website visitors who take a desired action. In Clyde's case, one of his goals is to sell more coffee. One way to see if his social media campaigns work is to watch conversion rates. For example, let's say Clyde sends out a coupon using Twitter. The coupon leads to a page on his website. He can count the number of users who clicked through from the Twitter link to the coupon's webpage in a variety of ways. Then, he can count the number of people who actually used the coupon in his café.

Wrapping Up

If Clyde does all these things—if *you* do all these things—will you sell more? I can't guarantee that. But I can guarantee this: If your product is something people want (in our example, if Clyde's coffee actually tastes good), and your place is nice, and your staff are friendly, that will help. If you are all these things online, too, where a growing majority of your customers are hanging out daily? That will help bring people back for more of what you do naturally, which is provide a great product or service.

So, start already. Start creating face2face connections with customers—just like you do in your store, your business, or your organization. People will think of you as a friend and will keep coming back for more.

APPENDIX

Referenced Websites and Social Media Services

Chapter 2

Skype, www.skype.com
Chris Brogan, www.chrisbrogan.com
Bill Marriott's Blog, blogs.marriott.com
Topeka & Shawnee County Public Library, www.tscpl.org
DavidLeeKing.com, www.davidleeking.com
ProBlogger, www.problogger.net
Facebook, www.facebook.com
Twitter, www.twitter.com
Foursquare, www.foursquare.com

Chapter 3

Flickr, www.flickr.com
YouTube, www.youtube.com
Google Maps, www.maps.google.com

Chapter 4

Think Big Topeka, www.thinkbigtopeka.com
American Library Association, www.ala.org
Ravelry, www.ravelry.com
ALA Connect, connect.ala.org
Basecamp, www.basecamphq.com

Chapter 5

Technorati, www.technorati.com
Google Blog Search, www.blogsearch.google.com
BackType, www.backtype.com
Topix, www.topix.net
Zappos, www.zappos.com
Twitter Search, www.search.twitter.com
BoardTracker, www.boardtracker.com
BoardReader, www.boardreader.com
Omgili, www.omgili.com
Google Groups, www.groups.google.com
Yahoo! Groups, www.groups.yahoo.com
FriendFeed, www.friendfeed.com
LinkedIn, www.linkedin.com
Tumblr, www.tumblr.com
Postling, www.postling.com
Addictomatic, www.addictomatic.com
Social Mention, www.socialmention.com
Digg, www.digg.com

TweetDeck, www.tweetdeck.com
HootSuite, www.hootsuite.com
Seesmic, www.seesmic.com
Spiral16, www.spiral16.com
Radian6, www.radian6.com
Viralheat, www.viralheat.com

Chapter 8

Google Reader, www.reader.google.com
Alexa, www.alexa.com

Chapter 11

Twitter Counter, www.twittercounter.com
TweetStats, www.tweetstats.com
Google Analytics, www.google.com/analytics

Chapter 12

Yelp, www.yelp.com

ABOUT THE AUTHOR

David Lee King is the digital services director at the Topeka & Shawnee County (Kansas) Public Library, where he plans, implements, and experiments with emerging technology trends. He has spoken at information industry events internationally about emerging tech trends, website usability and management, digital experience design and planning, and managing tech staff. He has been published in numerous library industry journals and, with Michael Porter, writes the "Outside/In" column in *American Libraries* magazine.

David is the chair of the board of directors for the Information Network of Kansas, and *Library Journal* named David a "Mover & Shaker" for 2008. David writes a popular blog that focuses on emerging tech trends, tips, and tools at www.davidleeking.com.

Before discovering his niche in the information industry, David held many jobs, including pizza delivery dude, customer service representative at a mutual fund company, housepainter, disc jockey, and freelance recording engineer. When not working, writing, or speaking, David enjoys writing songs and creating videos, as well as spending time with his amazing wife and his three cool kids.

David Lee King
blog: www.davidleeking.com
videoblog: www.davidleeking.tumblr.com
twitter | skype: davidleeking

INDEX

More Great Books from Information Today, Inc.

Designing the Digital Experience

How to Use Experience Design Tools and Techniques to Build Websites Customers Love

By David Lee King

Today's marketers and site designers can harness the power of "experience design" to help customers quickly find information, make purchases, or participate. *Library Journal* "Mover & Shaker" David Lee King explains the concepts behind designing digital experiences, describes a range of new tools and techniques, and shares experience design best practices.

224 pp/softbound/ISBN 978-0-910965-83-5 $39.95

The Mobile Marketing Handbook, 2nd Edition

A Step-by-Step Guide to Creating Dynamic Mobile Marketing Campaigns

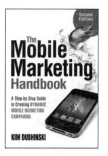

By Kim Dushinski

In this new interactive edition of her bestselling guide to mobile marketing, Kim Dushinski shows how any firm can create successful mobile campaigns without breaking the bank. Her easy-to-follow advice helps readers interact with mobile users, build stronger customer relationships, reach a virtually unlimited number of new prospects, and gain competitive advantage by making the move to mobile *now*.

248 pp/softbound/ISBN 978-0-910965-80-3 $29.95

Excellence Every Day

Make the Daily Choice—Inspire Your Employees and Amaze Your Customers

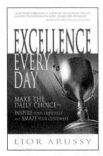

By Lior Arussy

If mediocre performance or results are acceptable at any level within your organization, this may be the most important book you will read this year. Lior Arussy explores and offers a solution to the root problem that keeps firms from delighting customers and inspiring superior performance and job satisfaction among employees. The "Excellence Myth" is a subtle yet pervasive mindset that undermines individual performance, erodes customer loyalty, and erases any competitive advantage a firm may enjoy or hope to gain. Arussy's inspired (and inspiring) remedy is the "Daily Choice," a strategy that empowers employees to reach new heights of excellence—creating delightful customer experiences and achieving superior results from the bottom up.

192 pp/softbound/ISBN 978-0-910965-79-8 $24.95

CRM in Real Time

Empowering Customer Relationships

By Barton J. Goldenberg

This guide to customer relationship management (CRM) shows how the right mix of people, process, and technology can help firms achieve a superior level of customer satisfaction, loyalty, and new business. *CRM in Real Time* covers a full range of critical issues, including integration challenges and security concerns, and illuminates CRM's key role in the 24/7/365 real-time business revolution.

384 pp/softbound/ISBN 978-0-910965-80-4 $39.95

Dancing With Digital Natives
Staying in Step With the Generation That's Transforming the Way Business Is Done

Edited by Michelle Manafy and Heidi Gautschi

Generational differences have always influenced how business is done, but in the case of digital natives—those immersed in digital technology from birth—we are witnessing a tectonic shift. Here, Michelle Manafy, Heidi Gautschi, and a stellar assemblage of experts from business and academia provide an in-depth look at how digital natives work, shop, play and learn, along with practical advice geared to help managers, marketers, coworkers, and educators maximize their interactions and create environments where everyone wins.

408 pp/hardbound/ISBN 978-0-910965-87-3 $27.95

UContent
The Information Professional's Guide to User-Generated Content

By Nicholas G. Tomaiuolo

Have you ever reviewed a book at Amazon.com? Uploaded a photo to Flickr? Commented on a blog posting? Used tags to describe or access information? If you have, you've contributed user-generated content (UContent) to the web. But while some librarians and information professionals have accepted their roles as creators and managers UContent, many have not. This comprehensive text considers the reasons behind UContent's wild popularity and makes strong arguments for cultivating it. *UContent* is a well researched book that serves as an overview, a status report, a primer, and a prognostication.

360 pp/softbound/ISBN 978-1-57387-425-0 $49.50